THE MILLION DOLLAR SALE

THE MILLION DOLLAR SALE

How to Get to the Top Decision Makers and Close the Big Sale in Just Two Calls

PATRICIA H. GARDNER
WITH TIMOTHY HAAS

McGraw-Hill

New York   Chicago   San Francisco   Lisbon   London
Madrid   Mexico City   Milan   New Delhi   San Juan
Seoul   Singapore   Sydney   Toronto

The McGraw·Hill Companies

1 2 3 4 5 6 7 8 9 0   DOC/DOC   0 1 0 9 8 7 6 5 4

ISBN 0-07-144519-6

This publication is designed to provide accurate and authoritative information in regard to the subject matter covered. It is sold with the understanding that neither the author nor the publisher is engaged in rendering legal, accounting, or other professional service. If legal advice or other expert assistance is required, the services of a competent professional person should be sought.

> —*From a Declaration of Principles jointly adopted by Committee of the American Bar Association and a Committee of Publishers.*

McGraw-Hill books are available at special quantity discounts to use as premiums and sales promotions, or for use in corporate training programs. For more information, please write to the Director of Special Sales, McGraw-Hill Professional, Two Penn Plaza, New York, NY 10121-2298. Or contact your local bookstore.

 This book is printed on recycled, acid-free paper containing a minimum of 50% recycled, de-inked fiber.

Library of Congress Cataloging-in-Publication Data

Gardner, Patricia.
    The million dollar sale : how to get to the top decision makers and close the big sale in just two calls / by Patricia Gardner ; with Timothy Haas.
       p. cm.
    Includes index.
    ISBN 0-07-144519-6 (alk. paper)
    1. Selling.   2. Business networks.   I. Haas, Timothy.   II. Title.
HF5438.25.G372   2005
658.85—dc22

                                                  2004016727

To all the hard-working salespeople out there looking for your big break—this book is for you!

Contents

Foreword

When I was senior account manager for global accounts at Sun Microsystems—the last position I held before retiring after more than 40 years in sales—a large part of my job was traveling to our local and regional offices around the world to help our sales representatives find and close high-dollar-volume sales by setting up partnerships and alliances. To make sure my reps reached their ambitious goals, I drew extensively on fast-paced, team-oriented techniques formulated by Patricia Gardner—techniques I had been privileged to witness in action. I'm thrilled that she's now sharing these methods with sales professionals everywhere in *The Million-Dollar Sale*.

One day back in the mid-1990s, during my assignment as Sun's senior pharmaceutical rep handling the Johnson & Johnson conglomerate, Pat called me and asked me to lunch. She was working for a systems integrator, selling consulting services—a brutally competitive market, but one, as her presentation to me made clear, that she understood perfectly. Always on the lookout for companies whose products or services could complement my own hardware and software in potentially providing turnkey solutions for my accounts, I readily agreed to meet with her.

As we sat there, exchanging information about our product capabilities and services and how hers might apply to my current accounts and other business possibilities I knew at J&J, I could tell Pat had something in mind. Through her research, she'd found out that J&J, a worldwide powerhouse consisting of more than 200 companies, didn't have an enterprise-level system tying all of their offices and divisions together. She wanted to talk to someone with the authority and the budget to undertake such a far-ranging project, and she wanted to do it before any competitors got the same idea. She made me a fair offer: "If you take me in, I'll make sure you get a shot at one of my biggest accounts."

It happened that I had an appointment coming up with a likely contact, so I brought her along. Now, when you're trying to win big sales, you don't just drop in for a chat. An information technology chief or corporate vice president doesn't want you poking behind the curtain trying to find out his needs. If you're not coming in with an idea that will increase his profits or decrease his operating costs, he doesn't want to see you. This type of call requires three times as much preparation as a typical sales call—and Pat really did her homework. She pitched an elegant solution for an intranet problem this executive was dealing with—a small job, to be sure, but one that her team wrapped up quickly, garnering her company instant credibility at J&J. After that, it didn't take her long to win the much larger project she'd been aiming for.

In a little more than a year of partnering, we completed four projects for a total of $7 million in revenue, and after two years we'd done nine projects and more than $15 million total—some with my clients, some with hers. Years of investigation and analysis of every aspect of the sales and service cycle crystallized in our joint success—I was her first Codebreaker, helping her reach the top decision makers in new accounts right out of the gate. She continued to use and refine this high-speed, high-stakes sales formula for the rest of her career, naturally becoming a formidable Codebreaker herself. Now, through her consulting business and speaking work, she's bringing the knowledge to a new generation of sales reps.

In *The Million Dollar Sale*, she lays out every step of the process you'll have to follow to secure a quota-busting deal, no matter what kind of product or service you're selling. After making a convincing case for the need to adopt a team sales approach, she tells readers how to put together flawless product presentations, assemble and manage unstoppable tactical teams, find new leads by tapping into every contact list at your company, keep complex projects on track while continuing the hunt for new business, and communicate effectively and genuinely with everyone from delivery guys all the way up to the CEO.

In between the broad strategic strokes, she also tips readers off to the little things that can speed the sales process and even turn a failing call around. Once you start to realize the scalability of what Pat calls three-dimensional thinking, you'll never dismiss any business goal as unattainable again.

I won't mislead you—to attract the interest of quality Codebreakers and prepare for the pressures of big-money sales, you're going to have to work hard and spend more preparation time than you ever have in your professional life. But once you've put Pat's ideas into practice, built your team, and gained your first win with a Codebreaker, the multiplier effect of successful partnering will kick in: Every participant in the deal will be searching out new opportunities to put together your next winning team. Your competition won't have a chance!

—Nick DeSilvis, retired Senior
Account Manager for Global
Accounts, Sun Microsystems

Acknowledgments

For their encouragement, thoughts, ideas, and suggestions, I would like to thank my daughter, Madeline Patricia Advani; my husband, Richard Reedinger; my father, Dr. Randolph S. Gardner; my mother, Madeleine Hayes Gardner; my sister, Dr. Madeleine Gardner; and my brother, Scott Gardner, and his wife, Dottie Gardner.

I'd also like to thank my first Codebreaker, Nick DeSilvis, who taught me that if you think you can't get the job done, you're just not working hard enough, because there is always a way.

I will be forever grateful to Timothy Haas for his collaboration and efforts in helping me translate my thoughts and spoken words into a readable format.

Introduction

In my 30 years of selling, one word has never been far from my mind: *speed*. When I started in 1973, my head was crammed full of the speeds of the Xerox copiers I was trying to place in every public and parochial school in Philadelphia. By the early 1980s, it was the ever-rising processing speed of the computers I was selling in Canada. And by the mid-1990s, what commanded my attention was the speed with which the consulting firm I was working for could design and implement solutions for IT clients at Fortune 500 companies.

But to my employers, only one speed ever mattered: how quickly I could close the next deal. It's always been that way, right? Well, let this veteran tell you something—in today's tight business climate, the pressure to close fast is even greater than it used to be. When's the last time you called a formal client meeting to sign a new contract? Grab a pen, get the signature, stick it in the fax machine, and move on! In this environment, we no longer have the time to cultivate layers of middle management in hopes of someday reaching the real decision makers. We have to start and finish at the top—every time.

In the course of my career, all the books I've read and all the seminars I've attended have concentrated on bolstering confidence and improving sales technique—worthy goals, to be sure, but nowhere near as crucial as being able to consistently get productive appointments with vice presidents and CIOs. Because, really, the right solution at the right time will always sell itself. The trick is finding the opportunities and putting yourself in a position to provide that solution, ideally in just two sales calls within a 30-day period.

And that's where Codebreakers come in.

The Codebreaker Concept

I'll give you a more detailed definition later, but to put it simply, a Codebreaker is someone, usually a sales rep outside of your company, who is already writing millions of dollars' worth of business annually with one of your potential clients.

My first Codebreaker was a former Xerox colleague who had moved to a leading computer company. He was selling tens of millions of dollars of hardware each year to select pharmaceutical companies. I was working for a systems integrator, and when I found out that his company didn't sell consulting services, I offered to team up with him: If he would help me crack a pharmaceutical account, I would get him into one of our clients. Well, our first collaboration was so successful, we just kept rolling. We did more than $7 million in deals together in a 12-month period.

After this, I realized that partnering with an established vendor on a specific project is the surest path to the first big deal with a new client. You're trading in part on someone else's reputation to get in the door, and adding to it when your job comes in on time and on budget and does even more than you promised.

Once I consciously made it part of my approach, I started finding Codebreakers for every major account I was trying to penetrate. As you can probably imagine, though, Codebreakers aren't just hanging out at the water cooler waiting to be pitched. These are supremely busy people who have achieved their high status by proving their value to clients over and over again. Before you even think of trying to enlist a Codebreaker's help, you have to know your product and market and be ready to demonstrate how you're going to bring something fresh to his client.

Preparation over Salesmanship

For many people, the biggest surprise about closing huge deals in a short time is that it has very little to do with salesmanship and everything to do with preparation. Don't get me wrong, the polish never hurts—but don't we all know at least a handful of colleagues who could sell a handbag to an alligator but who nonetheless seem to end up alienating customers because they don't actually solve problems?

The kind of preparation I'm talking about isn't just knowing your product and market. It's taking care of your support staff so they'll be ready to back you up when you're in a tight spot. It's developing an in-house tactical team who can respond quickly when you get the go-ahead for a proposal and who keep their eyes open while on other jobs for new leads. It's keeping up on the latest innovations so that you have something of value to offer every time you contact a potential client or Codebreaker.

But perhaps the most important preparation you can make is wrapping your mind around what might be a whole new approach to selling.

Think or Sink

One of the first things you were probably told on your first job was "Never give up. Make 10 more calls, knock on 20 more doors till you get a sale." Well, I beg to differ. "Any sale is a good sale"—that's the small-timer's fallback.

When you're running up against a wall, you shouldn't be asking yourself "How much harder do I have to push?" Instead, you should be thinking of ways to scale the wall. Eventually, this way of thinking will change your entire method—you'll have gone from a sales orientation to a thought-process orientation, one of the key elements of finding and closing quota-busting deals.

To illustrate this, let me tell you a quick story. When I first moved up to Canada to sell for Xerox, I loved to work on what we called "zero population" accounts—companies that for one reason or another had no Xerox equipment at all, and accordingly represented both a great challenge and a great opportunity to be a hero. One of the most interesting to land on my desk was Goodyear

Canada, a national company that had shot down some of our best reps. That folder sat there for two months because I kept thinking, "Really good people haven't been able to get any business out of there—how am I going to?"

I knew nothing about tires; I didn't even know anything about cars. All I really had were some notes from the other reps. After consulting some resources to get a handle on the company, I noticed in the parking lot one day that all of the technicians had Goodyears on their vans. So I called our corporate headquarters in Toronto and said, "How many cars do we have leased?" I found out we had about 2200 GM cars—every one of which had Goodyear tires.

Now, I knew from the notes that Goodyear had one or two huge Kodak copying units, along with a lot of smaller offshore equipment. I asked my contact at corporate whether he had an idea of how many GM cars Kodak leased. To this day I don't know how he knew this, but he was able to tell me straight off that they had only 275 cars. So I called Goodyear and made an appointment.

I met with a gruff but receptive gentleman whose pride in his company was obvious. I asked him to tell me a little bit about where Goodyear ranked in the industry, and after throwing out some impressive statistics about their quality, he began to tell me how offshore manufacturers had come in during the 1970s and copied all of Goodyear's technology. Their own tools were now being used to undercut their market position.

"That's exactly what happened to us at Xerox," I said.

He looked at me with sympathy. "I know," he said. "Those guys *are* cheaper than you."

This is where the homework paid off. "You know," I continued, "that's two things we have in common—that and our partnership."

He shook his head. "Partnership? But I don't have any of your equipment."

"I know, but *we* have"—and I pulled out the fax from the fellow in corporate—"2200 GM cars with Goodyear tires." His eyes started to get wide. "And I know you have this huge Kodak machine—did you know that they only have 275 cars?"

"Oh, my gosh."

"There's only one problem with this partnership," I said. "It's very one-sided."

Well, it didn't take him long to clear out that Kodak unit and all of the offshore copiers and replace them all with Xerox equipment. In this instance, he didn't save a dime, because we *were* more expensive—but we brought something to the relationship that none of the other vendors could. By helping to modify your strategic approach, I hope to do the same for you.

How to Use This Book

Though you can apply its lessons in any kind of industry, from durable equipment to consulting vaporware, *The Million Dollar Sale* is not a book for beginners. I assume that you know the basics of selling and probably have been in the field for at least a few years. However, the first four chapters are a strategic refresher course that—if you need it—can help you:

- Gain a deeper knowledge of your product or service (or learn a new one) in a short time.

- Identify your competition and get a handle on their strengths and weaknesses.

- Figure out your vertical market (especially useful for smaller companies that need to concentrate on a specific niche to be able to grow).

- Find and use various resources to name potential customers in your vertical.

If you already have a solid command of your product and market, you can skip ahead to Chapter 5, "Finding Your Codebreakers." This chapter and Chapter 6 will expose the secrets of uncovering potential Codebreakers among colleagues, clients, and even neighbors, and show you how to nurture a relationship that will benefit both of you.

Maybe you'll realize after reading the definition of a Codebreaker that you already know someone—maybe more than one someone, if you've been an active networker—who fits the parameters. Turn straight to the heart of the book to master these details of finding and closing million-dollar deals in two sales calls:

- Developing three potential projects before meeting your potential client—and how to adjust if those don't fly.

- Letting the Codebreaker take the lead on the first sales call—and don't forget to debrief immediately after.

- Doing a reality check with your in-house team to make sure you'll be able to provide the solution the client needs.

- Getting the customer's influencers on your side.

- Bringing in the heavy hitters for the second sales call—and getting ready to hash out the final proposal.

- Nailing down the details in a conference call as the time for the close draws near.

Each chapter ends with a checklist you can use to mark your progress and, down the line, refresh your memory of the book's core concepts. Although the most recent portion of my career was spent in IT consulting and software sales, I have drawn on my extensive product selling and sales training experience to provide real-life examples applicable to every industry and every kind of sales. Take what you need to succeed!

If You're a Sales Manager

I urge you to use the opportunity this book provides to take a hard look at your sales culture. If you're blessed with a motivated, well-adjusted sales force already meeting or exceeding their goals, think of it as a source of new ideas that you can fit to your style. After all, who couldn't benefit from an extra 5 percent on top of already big numbers? But if you're mired in a slump, with disappointing quarterlies and unhappy reps, consider this a roadmap to a more efficient, more productive way of doing things.

The two distinguishing elements of the Codebreaker approach are *preparation* and *teamwork*. Too often, sales reps aren't given enough—or any—time to research new accounts or even their own product lines, which results in flawed presentations and wasted chances. When hiring a new rep or transferring someone to a new product or vertical market, build in a couple of weeks of pure learning time. If you're selling a tangible good or hardware and software, encourage the rep to put the product through its paces and talk to members of the design and service staffs. If you're a consulting or service organization, try to arrange interviews with satisfied clients—they'll give the rep an unvarnished view of what your company was able to accomplish for them.

After the rep has learned the ropes and is out there selling, recognize that certain clients and projects might require additional prep time. The Codebreaker approach is more results-oriented than process-oriented—it's not about initiating contact with a certain number of prospects every week, but about going after the contacts most likely to result in big new business. This might upset the established order in your shop, but it's worth the effort.

Developing a teamwork ethic might be a little harder, especially if competition has been the main motivator for your staff. You've got to lower the barriers between sales and other departments. Engineers might not be salespeople, but some of them might be able to sell a certain aspect of your product better than a team of the slickest reps—encourage their supervisors to let them come along to client meetings when the stakes are high. Give senior people responsibility for junior reps—make a portion of their bonuses dependent on proving that they've helped open a certain number of doors. Use this book's many examples of the financial rewards of teamwork to convince a reluctant staff.

You can start using the Codebreaker approach with just one of your reps, though I suggest that you try it with two or three to increase cross-selling opportunities. These methods are addictive, and once part of the staff is up to speed, the possibilities will start coming from everywhere. Say a rep develops a Codebreaker who has access to channels outside of the rep's core area—why wouldn't you want to have another team member ready to step in and keep the opportunity alive?

Something else I'd like you to give serious thought to: making a formal compensation plan for Codebreakers both inside *and outside* your company. Codebreakers can open the doors to literally millions of dollars of business—reward them not only with reciprocal business opportunities, but with financial incentives as well. Isn't a million-dollar deal worth a $5000 or $10,000 finder's fee? It might not be the way things have been done in the past, but it just makes good business sense.

THE MILLION DOLLAR SALE

The Four Fundamentals of Sales

The First Fundamental: Knowing Your Product or Service

Sports commentators always like to talk about *fundamentals*—the basic competencies someone needs to have mastered to be called a professional. The fundamentals of sales are interpersonal—knowing how to talk to people persuasively while handling objections and displaying enthusiasm for your product or service.

To write million-dollar deals, of course, these fundamentals have to be flawless—as much a part of you as your voice and body language, whether by gift of personality or plain hard work. But don't forget that every new job brings an additional set of fundamentals that you must adopt thoroughly but quickly, the most important of which is figuring out just what it is you're going to be selling.

The overall process of learning to sell single-function tangible goods such as boilers is slightly different from learning to sell multifunction items like computer hardware—but both of them are very different from learning to sell strategic consulting services. I think two weeks is enough time to learn any new product well enough to start selling it effectively, while hard-won experience tells me it can take months to really understand everything a broad-based systems integrator can do. (More on that, and consulting services in general, later in the chapter.)

Many larger companies offer boot camps to give new reps the sales and technical grounding they need to start making calls. I went through such a program myself back in the 1970s at Xerox, and I wouldn't have traded it for the world. But let's assume your company doesn't offer one. How do you ensure that you give yourself effective training in a short time? And what if you're taking on a type of product or service that you've never sold before? I'm going to show you how to take control of your training and make connections throughout your company who will support you later in the field.

Step One: Convincing Your Boss

In the Introduction, we talked about the tight business climate. Today, you're hired and your boss says, "The clock starts right now." I tell my sales consulting clients that they should give a new salesperson 60 days to get comfortable before imposing a quota, but most just won't do it. Even if you're not allowed that breathing room, there are things you and your sales manager can do together in those first few weeks to increase your likelihood of success.

It's possible that a really good manager will suggest some of these things on his own, but chances are that you're going to have to plant the seed yourself. Think of this conversation as just another sales call. You're persuading the boss to let you direct your own training in a structured way that he might not be accustomed to overseeing, but that will pay off handsomely. Here are my suggested talking points:

Helping me set up a checklist of what I need to know will ensure that I hit all the high points without taking up a lot of your time.

It's a pretty good bet that the sales manager already knows what a typical rep needs to internalize to be effective on a particular product. But during those hectic first weeks on the job, who knows what her schedule is going to be like? Getting it all down on paper at the outset gives you goals to shoot for and gives her a convenient set of benchmarks. Properly critiqued and updated, it will also prove an excellent resource for future trainees.

Meeting with the technical and marketing staff will teach me more about my key product than just reading the manual.

The techies know all the quirks and all the shortcuts, and, most important, they know how customers really use the product. You should consider it mandatory to spend some time with at least one technical person and one marketing staff member.

Arranging for me to have a little time with administrative staffers will help me understand our billing and fulfillment process, so that I can head off customer problems before they occur.

Here's another group of hardworking folks who don't always get their due from the sales staff, but who handle two of the most important jobs in the company—making sure the product gets to the customer and collecting the money! Plus, commission structures, especially in the consulting world, are arcane and prone to error—it helps to have someone on the inside when one of those mistakes happens to you.

After talking with current customers, I will have a much better command of the requirements of my market.

Every company should do this: Find three customers who have bought within the last few months, bring them in, feed them lunch, and find out why they chose you over your competitors and what it's going to take to keep their business. If the schedules don't mesh, go to them—they're too important a resource to skip.

Traveling with experienced reps will help me tie all these strands together and improve my technique.

Nothing works better in training than sharing with someone who has sold your product successfully. You can avoid months of mistakes with just a few days' effort. If you're replacing someone who's been promoted, for example, suggest that a mentoring relationship could benefit both of you.

If you're lucky and have a sharp sales manager, he'll understand your request and immediately be able to suggest a possible mentor, the right techs to talk to, likely customers to approach. He should make the initial calls, or—even better—introduce you personally to each kind of contact, stressing how much you're looking forward to working with them and their teams. For one reason or another, not all may be willing to assist you, but a gracious reaction to this rejection will serve you well if you do end up working together at some point.

Now that you've laid the groundwork for your program, let's look at each element in detail.

Step Two: Covering the Basics

Plan on spending the first week of your training period getting comfortable with the capabilities of your product or products. But that doesn't mean diving right into the user manuals and spec sheets.

What I recommend first is focusing on the product's benefit to the customer. What service does it provide? Does it offer a specific solution or add value to another solution?

For an example, let's look at copiers, where I started out. They don't do anything fancy—they make black marks on white paper. But what do those black marks on white paper allow the customer to do? Disseminate information very quickly. So, speed is an essential aspect of this product. Part of keeping up that speed is reliability, which is achieved mainly by selecting a piece of equipment with the proper copying capacity. What are the limits of this machine? When should I think about looking at a more advanced model? By thinking like a customer—starting not with the general numbers, but with the requirements that will lead us to specific numbers—we've gained insight into his experience, improving and streamlining our approach. At the end of this exercise, you'll know what to concentrate on when you're spending the time to get physically comfortable with the equipment and what sections of the manual you can skim so that you're ready for that lone customer down the line who wants to hear about every little detail.

And though it isn't likely to happen in your first two weeks, if you're ever given the chance to get your hands dirty with your customers' work, by all means take it. A few years into my career at Xerox, I became a 9200 specialist. The 9200s were revolutionary machines, a whole print shop in one monster-size package. One of my big prospects was a local Army print shop, a market populated with offset pressmen.

Calling on these guys, I learned that customers will sometimes lie. The guy who ran the shop kept telling me my numbers were wrong. It wasn't malicious, really—he and his men had invested a lifetime in their craft and were understandably nervous about the automation of their jobs even as they sniffed at the trade-off between speed and quality. But it was a government account—I knew the numbers. I had to prove to him I knew he was fudging. So

I actually went out and learned how to run an offset press. I didn't become an expert by any means, but I knew the job well enough to point out when he was straying from the truth. And it worked—I eventually put *two* 9200s in that shop. It was great training, and a great lesson: No matter how much they try, salespeople will never know their customers' needs as well as the customer, but they should have enough of a grasp to be able to challenge customer assertions.

Step Three: Talking with Your Internal Customers

At the beginning of your second week, you're going to a take a little break from chipsets and flow controls to address a different but equally crucial topic: your relationship with people throughout the company. You're going to meet with colleagues from various departments to map out how you can help one another toward common goals: customer satisfaction and increased revenue. A savvy salesperson will think of his coworkers as internal customers because they can make or break a sale as surely as an external customer.

Whatever their role, you should consider each one a respected equal. You're new to the company and can use all the help they can give you. Recognize that they're busy and honor their time by showing up when you're supposed to and listening keenly. Take them to lunch if you both have the time. The working relationships you can foster in these early days will increase your happiness when things are going great and support you when things seem as if they're falling down around you.

If one of your new colleagues has been especially helpful, follow up with a typed letter on letterhead—not an e-mail—to his boss. One service person I worked with whose supervisor got one of those letters said, "You know, I've worked here 30 years and nobody has ever done that." On a late Friday afternoon in August, he had waited on a dock in 100-degree heat for my equipment to be delivered. He didn't have to stick around—if equipment isn't delivered on time, they're off to the next job. But he knew it was important for the company and it was important to me to get that equipment delivered and installed that day. He stayed long past 5:00 to get the job done. That's a company guy. By showing the proper appreciation when someone has gone out of his way for you, you'll help to build more company-minded people.

Let's look at the meetings you should definitely set up.

The Techies or Service Representatives

It's an unfortunate fact that a lot of technical and service represen-tatives think of salespeople as self-promoters who sweet-talk cus-tomers but treat their own staff rudely. New salespeople sometimes think, "Oh, well, they just write code or fix machines," but technical staffers and service people actually spend more time with your cus-tomers than you do. No matter what their title—project manager, engineer, systems integrator, service representative, help-desk rep, technician, product specialist, repairman—they are a great resource for sales professionals in every industry, and it's up to you to set the tone of the relationship by being open, friendly, and gen-uinely curious about them and their responsibilities.

One time at Xerox, I was having difficulty getting a downtown Philadelphia law firm to upgrade to a higher-capacity machine. Trying to get some insight, I sought out the technician who handled the account. He was a natural, able to give me a detailed but clear explanation of the specific features the client needed in the new machine. Realizing I couldn't let this chance go by, I asked if he would come to the demo room and repeat his performance for the customer. I was definitely breaking tradition—I even had to get permission from his boss to take him into the field with me—but the client, who already trusted the tech's work, listened raptly while he demonstrated the advantages of the new equipment over the current machine. It was without a doubt one of the easiest sales I ever made, and after that a lot of my colleagues started integrating tech folks into their sales process.

Early in your second week of prep work is a perfect time to talk with these experts, once you can demonstrate the product's basic capabilities and rattle off reliability numbers. Your tech will help you refine your presentation by providing a reality check: "I know the manuals say that, but in the field here's what we've found." Or, "That particular feature you emphasized in your pitch does seem important, but actually, customers rarely use it. You should consider talking about this feature instead." You can also ask if the technical staff likes hearing feedback from sales reps that they can pass along to the engineers and designers.

Some of them are naturally going to lapse into tech-speak, just as you might employ sales jargon at a rep meeting. Don't panic— take it all in, then come back to the points you feel you need to understand better and ask for a simpler explanation. You're really doing this for two reasons: to increase your own knowledge and to give the tech a kind of audition. As we'll see in Chapter 3, you're going to be creating a tactical team you'll be able to rely on in the heat of the deal, and it's an immense help to have techs who can break down complex topics into layman's terms. For this reason, try to meet with two or three techs if you can, in hopes of finding one who has as good a presence in front of customers as that old Xerox tech of mine.

You might or might not, of course, have a choice about which tech or group of techs you talk to, especially if the service department is based on geography. If it seems as if you're not going to be a good fit, you can always ask him to recommend other people to talk to.

Administrative Staff and Delivery People

Once you're rolling in your territory, you're not going to see the administrative folks as often as you are the techs, but they're just as important to your success. I like to go around and meet the people who create the pricing for a product. It also helps to meet the sales executives and get a sense of the culture: What is required of me as a sales rep? If I have a quota, what do they expect me to do in the first 30, 60, 90 days, and how much support am I going to get? Should I ask the sales manager to travel with me? Does the president ever come out and meet clients?

I need to know how products and services are billed and how I'll be compensated. If I'm not credited until after the customer has paid the bill, I'd like to know how it's tracked and how often I'll be copied in on that information so that I can check it against my own records. The best salespeople in the world keep track of every deal they close and review commissions due on a monthly and quarterly basis.

If you're taking over a territory from another rep, you should make sure the system knows to credit you, rather than the old rep, with new commissions. Being faced with this situation once helped me uncover an even larger problem. I found that I wasn't being paid properly for commissions from a large and normally reliable client, and reviewed it with our internal sales compensation coordinator. It turned out that the client owed us hundreds of thousands of dollars, but we couldn't seem to collect. I phoned and made an appointment with their procurement department and said I'd like to go through all the invoices. When I walked in a few days later, they took me to a large conference room where'd they'd spread out every invoice for the past six months. We went through them one by one, turning up bad requisition forms, forms with the wrong vendor ID numbers, you name it—mainly the work of one of our sales reps who had mentally checked out a few months before he physically retired. My efforts resulted in our company being paid nearly half a million dollars within a couple of days, and I saw that knowing the important facts about my company's procedures had really made a frustrating task go much more smoothly.

Make sure you treat the controllers and accountants well. Chances are they were stomped on at some point by a rep who didn't get paid properly, and they might be wary. You want to hear the strengths and weaknesses of the system: "You need to be aware that sometimes there are mistakes on this form. We usually catch them within a few days." Or, "If you don't file this report on time, payment won't go through."

When it comes to the delivery staff, just introducing yourself can be a big boost. When they can put a friendly face to a name on the shipping manifest, you're going to get more consideration. More than once delivery guys have gone out of their way to help me when the situation on the ground wasn't up to the terms of the contract—a space wasn't laid out properly, or they were denied access to an entrance large enough to fit the equipment. Instead of just packing up and leaving someone else to sort out the problem, as they're technically allowed to do, they'd call me on my cell and give me the time I needed to get it fixed for them. That kind of rapport is priceless to your commission revenue.

Step Four: Meeting Some "Friendlies"

If you want to test your assumptions about how customers use your product, go for the real deal—bring them in, put out a nice spread, and interview them. One of my old firms did this all the time, and the clients loved it. Their good feelings about your company are reinforced—it's amazing how many companies never even really say thank you to clients—and you get to ask basic questions that might seem too naïve in a regular sales call: Why did you pick our product over another product? What did you like about it? What did you dislike? How important was the pricing? Was it just that it fit in a particular place? You'd be amazed what some of the answers are—it might have absolutely nothing to do with salesmanship, but just that the product fulfilled a particular need on a particular day. Some of the sales you close aren't always about how brilliant you were that day, even though some salespeople like to think that.

This kind of information pays off in the long run as well. Six months later when you're on a sales call and a customer is saying "Your products are too expensive," you can counter with "That's exactly what Fred Johnson from ABC Company said about us. But he told us that he still bought from us because he realized that the upgrades on this other product that you're looking at were going to cost more over the life of the product. So, in actuality, our price turns out to be less."

You can always learn something new from your "friendlies," and it's always important to see them. If they can't afford to spend half a day to come to you, see if you can get an hour at their office. Try to arrange at least three of these kinds of calls—four or five would be even better.

Step Five: Knowing When You Know Enough

At the end of the two weeks, you should know and be able to demonstrate the following things about your product during an office role-playing session:

- What are the core competencies of the product?
- What are the three key things the product does for your client base?
- How have other clients employed the product?

- What differentiates the product from others?

- What value does the product add to the client's business?

- What is the product's return on investment (ROI) for the client? How much will clients save by using the product, and how quickly will they realize it?

- What proof sources and metrics can you point to that will verify your claims?

If you can answer all of these questions comfortably, congratulations—you're ready to head out on some calls.

Step Six: Traveling with More Experienced Reps

Riding along with a senior sales rep on a series of calls is the capstone experience of your self-service boot camp—there's certainly no quicker way of honing your technique than watching a successful colleague in her element.

Beneficial as it will be, it could be the most difficult portion of the training to set up. You're going to need your sales manager to lay the groundwork. Why? Well, for one thing, a successful rep is busy—just getting a slot in her schedule could prove tough. And she might have to be sold on the idea that mentoring a junior rep will add to the perception around the office that she's management material.

But it really comes down to this: Even the most tenured salesperson is as nervous as a cat when she has somebody traveling with her. What if it turns out to be one of the bad days we all have from time to time? What if she slips up and says something she instantly regrets? It's up to you to put your colleague at ease at the start of the day. Open up to her a little bit—tell her what your goals are and ask her about her time with the company, what she thinks of the support staff. Assure her that everything's off the record, and keep your promise. By setting the right tone, you're going to allow her to relax and really give you targeted advice. And when you get back to the office, let the sales manager know just how talented you think the senior rep is and how valuable you found her attention.

After a few days like this, you'll be ready to strike out on your own. As you're making those first solo calls, you'll start the process covered in Chapter 2, identifying your competition—another crucial element to consider when you're shooting for million-dollar deals. (Note: If you're not involved in consulting, you can go straight to Chapter 2 and start researching your competitors.)

When You're Selling Services

Consulting services represent an immense opportunity. The work is fast-paced and exciting, the margins are fantastic, and your coworkers are truly the best and brightest. No project is the same—you're in the business of finding perfect solutions to very particular problems. You are entering the Land of the Million-Dollar Deal. But as you can imagine, a two-week boot-camp approach just isn't enough to learn your product here. Let me illustrate by telling you how I made the change from copiers to consulting.

As the tech boom was taking off in the mid-1990s, I realized it was time to wax up my surfboard and plunge in or I'd miss the wave. I left Xerox and moved to a systems integration firm to sell consulting services and Sun Microsystems hardware as a value-added reseller (VAR). The tricky part? I had no IT background and knew absolutely nothing about selling large-scale computer systems.

At the very beginning, I went to training courses for our different partner companies. Unlike in tangible product sales, I wasn't going to learn all the intricacies of Sun equipment from our technical people, either because not all of them sold those products or because they were so used to the product that they couldn't even communicate on my level. And the meetings! UNIX, Java, TCP/IP—I didn't understand a tenth of what was being said. But I sat there and took notes, and afterward I would buttonhole one of the participants to get the layman's version.

Eventually I developed a team of techies who were happy to come along with me on appointments, and business picked up rapidly. But there were times that I still had to go alone because once we started selling, the techs were all busy working on projects. One time I met with an extremely technical woman who assumed that I'd be able to keep up with her. She covered a white board with diagrams on the perfect project for us, and I didn't understand any of it. At the end of the meeting, she announced, "So, you need to put together a proposal for me."

I'm thinking, Ah, yes, absolutely. I hadn't taken enough notes. As calmly as I could, I said, "Do you have anything in writing?" And she pulled out a six-page report she had created for her boss to get permission to initiate the project—you can't imagine my relief. We got the job—but I never went to see her again without taking someone with me.

It took me the first 90 days to just barely keep my head above water, and six months to get comfortable. But after years of selling and training others to sell consulting services, I now think a motivated rep starting from scratch can learn the ropes in 30 days. But unless you have a technical mind, heed my lesson and take somebody with you—don't waste valuable time with customers by being unsure of what you can commit to.

To get up to effective selling speed, along with the steps described earlier in the chapter, you need to do the following:

- **Get the abridged version of each of your firm's proven strengths.** CRM, supply chain, e-procurement—meet with one person within each of these core competencies, even if you're not going to sell them, so that you understand the firm's big picture enough to do a corporate presentation and know when to pass business along to a different unit.

- **Study the cutoff levels between products, in terms of both price and capabilities, instead of trying to absorb every detail.** If you know item X is an entry-level product or service and item Y is the next step up, it lets you present clients with clear choices rather than a menu they have to think about.

- **Get the information you need to prove your value add, differentiator, and ROI.** Even when I was floundering around, I could nail these essential elements of a successful presentation. Press your sales manager for case studies of past projects and keep after the latest data from new projects.

- **Create your "go-to team."** Consultants are notorious for wanting every call "prequalified"—meaning essentially that the rep has already determined the potential client's budget and interest level for a certain project. You've got to keep networking within the company to find people who are open to working with you even when you call up and say, "I don't know if I have a perfect opportunity here, but I have an appointment next Thursday at 11 that I think will interest you." (More on this in Chapter 3.)

On to the competition!

Chapter Checklist

To learn your product quickly and efficiently, you have to:

☐ Convince your sales manager to give you a few weeks for a self-led boot camp.

☐ Dive into the basics of the product or service, concentrating on the benefits it provides to customers.

☐ Get to know your internal customers: engineers and other technical staff, service technicians, administrative and financial staff, delivery staff.

☐ Arrange to meet with some "friendlies"—satisfied customers who can give you insight into what your company has been doing right.

☐ Evaluate your new knowledge base to determine when enough is enough and it's time to start selling.

☐ Schedule travel days with more experienced reps to confirm your lessons and refine your approach.

☐ Make learning an ongoing process, especially if you're selling complex consulting services.

The Second Fundamental: Learning the Competition

You've mastered your product's fundamentals, introduced your-self to the support staff, even started to go out on a couple of unsupervised sales calls. Now begins the second phase of your basic education: developing an accurate picture of your competition and figuring out your strategic edge.

Before you start to compare feature lists and columns of stats, however, there is one thing you must take to heart: You will always have competition. At the risk of being annoying, I'm going to repeat that: You will *always* have competition. If you think otherwise, you are guaranteed to fail. Your company can produce the most earth-shaking product since penicillin, and three months down the road someone's going to do it cheaper or better. (Heaven help you if it's both.) And if by a miracle you do manage to avoid direct competi-tion, you still have competition from every other product and service out there.

Every day, all day long, your competition is calling your cus-tomers. You need to take a hard look at your product or company's core competencies and understand where and by whom they're going to be challenged. This doesn't mean you'll need to acquire ιe same depth of knowledge about competitors' products that you have about your first, but you do have to know how you stack up.

I'll give you an example. At one point late in my career, I was selling knowledge management software. Without a strong technical background I had no chance of fully understanding how such complex program suites worked, but the customer benefits were obvious. I needed to know just enough about the software to be able to figure out the strengths and weaknesses of the opposing players.

I discovered that some competing products were designed to offer alerts—notifications when new pieces of information became available on the company's system. We didn't have this capability, so I quickly realized I didn't have a chance in something like the financial market, where users need to be kept up-to-the-minute on things like stock price fluctuations. But, because my product had other advantages, I could do well in the pharmaceutical and life sciences industry, where they did not need an alert system. Finding this one crucial difference enabled me to target the right business segments for my product, eliminate a lot of potentially wasted time, and point out when a competitor's product might be overkill for my customers. (In fact, this is how I made one of my own million-dollar deals.)

What You Need to Find Out

You probably picked up some idea of who your main competitors are during your training period; it's one of the natural things reps talk about when they're together. If you're trying to take business away from a market leader, your sales manager will have filled you in. You might be seeing other firms' reps in the lobby. Even the sign-in book at the reception desk can be an info bonanza—who's been in to see your contact lately?

But, really, it's a piece of cake to draw up a list of competing firms. The hard work comes in making an accurate assessment of the strengths and weaknesses of your products and your competitors' as they relate to your customers' needs. It's hard to say what kind of differentiator—price, capabilities, quality of service, ease of maintenance, even the location of your headquarters—will most influence your clients; each of those elements is ripe for exploration. In my experience, almost everyone is interested in a solution that is as trouble-free as possible. Jumping through hoops takes time, and that costs money. You can expect questions such as: How much of my staff's time will be required? Will I have to rely on your people for the next six months until it's completely integrated into our system, or will my people be able to take it over quickly? If you sell a product that's easily integrated or offers trouble-free solutions, you know what areas to emphasize. (And if not, you know what to encourage the engineers to work on next.)

To get started, write down the names of your top three competitors and list *all* the features of their products, even ones that your product doesn't have—you need to be aware if you fall short somehow. Working from the full list, you should then be able to identify your product's five greatest strengths. Concentrating on these areas will give you plenty to talk about with a new customer and will also make for a great summary chart at the end of a corporate presentation. (See Figure 2.1.)

Other firms are, of course, going to do their best to minimize their weaknesses. You have to train yourself to look for what's not mentioned in their marketing materials and spec sheets—a glaring omission means they're trying to bury something.

Of course, it's human nature to underestimate a competitor's strengths and magnify its weaknesses in your own mind. No matter how excited you are about working for a new company or finally releasing a new product, you must avoid this key mistake. Somebody else is going to be better in certain areas—you can't be all things to all people with all products.

Figure 2.1   THREE COMPETITORS AND YOU

	MY PRODUCT	COMPETITOR #1	COMPETITOR #2	COMPETITOR #3
11 x 17	✓		✓	✓
Two-sided	✓	✓		✓
Automatic document feeder	✓	✓	✓	✓
Sorting	✓	✓	✓	
Stapling	✓			

I know it's going to take your getting banged around a few times, losing when you *knew* you had a win, before reality sets in. Believe me, I've been as guilty of it as anyone, so how can I blame you? But one thing I never did, even when I was mad at a loss, was to slam the competition. Mudslingers always fail, because that's not what the customer wants to hear. They want usable information about your product's superiority, not an ego trip.

Learning from Your Customers

Apart from simple business decorum, there's another reason not to alienate potential and current customers with negativity: If you listen closely, they'll teach you everything you need to know about your competition—and about being a more effective sales rep. I am going to give you some tips about publications-based research at the end of this chapter, but I've never been one for doing a lot of it. No matter how much I could gain by reading every line written by and about a competitor, it was always much quicker and more effective to let my customers cut to the core of the differences between us.

For example, if you survey the knowledge management software market, you'll find about 10 players. That seems like a stiff competitive field. But when you get a customer talking about the business solution he needs, seven will immediately fall off the board—one vendor doesn't have enough staff to deal with more than one large account, another never bids outside of its narrow segment, yet another is rumored to be in financial trouble. In the end, after a lot of tough decision making, customers generally consider only three firms seriously. These are brilliant people who understand their requirements 10 times better than a vendor ever will—accept their hard-won wisdom and follow their lead. If you're open with them— "How can I build a better product?"—they will respond.

You'll never get them to tell you all the specifics because a lot of what they're looking to accomplish is proprietary. But you know that they're looking for the best solutions, so you can draw your own conclusions when they say something like "We need a product that can handle a million hits per hour, and Company A's product missed the mark" (clearly speed is key) or "It did the job, but the quality metrics didn't measure up to our standards" (here, quality is the main concern). This is the kind of inside news you're never going to read in a white paper.

Product face-offs are also a great way to learn from your customers. If you're really good, you're never afraid to say, in a respectful and matter-of-fact way, "Let us bring it in and prove it to you." Smart customers get that done all the time, sometimes with a prototype but usually with a production unit. These 30- or 60-day trials generate priceless information, even if you ultimately lose. Those are the customers you should ask, "What is it about my product that made the difference?" Or, "Why did I lose to that particular competitor?" Most customers, for their own internal purposes, will have narrowed it down to a few particulars and will tell you precisely why you won or lost:

- "This is where your strengths are, and this is where your weaknesses are."

- "We needed a more robust solution to this particular problem."

- "This particular feature was more important to us than you assumed."

- "I didn't find out I needed a particular component that only your competitor offers until we got deeper into the project."

It might be hard to sit there and have your failures detailed like that, but it's imperative that you take it as the gift it is: The notes you bring away from that meeting will form the basis of your revised approach on your next sales call.

One time I was handling a lot of departments at the state of New Jersey for Xerox. The bill room at the state legislature had this huge copier from Kodak; we had gone up against them initially and lost. They must have been swayed by the other guy's salesmanship, because the product didn't do what they needed it to, and I knew it. But I continued to go in there to see how they were getting on with the machine and to ask about output and reliability. Of course it was somewhat exasperating to behold this inadequate machine where mine should have been, but by returning again and again, I learned more about the client's real needs and about my competitor's product. I later put both of those elements to good use—first by presenting a more accurate picture of the differences between my product and the competitor's at subsequent sales calls, and second by eventually getting my copier into the bill room. It also helped, of course, in other situations where I was going head-to-head with the same Kodak model.

I know it takes time, but if you make this kind of information collection an ongoing project, you'll soon build up a wonderful library of competitive knowledge that will save much more time down the road. It is absolutely essential to share this with your sales colleagues, and your technicians will benefit from it as well.

Additional Sources of Information

Let's say you haven't been able to develop much useful information from your customers because you're releasing a brand-new product, or maybe you need to get a basic handle on what you need to ask before you approach them. What are some other avenues to follow?

The Ringer

It pays to ask around the office to find out whether anyone on the staff used to work for a competitor in a relevant position—this is akin to being handed a golden egg.

Of course, some companies actively seek to buy these golden eggs: Many years ago at Xerox, we hired away a top-notch salesman from a leading office product company to be a trainer for us. He looked, acted, and played the part perfectly—expensive blue pinstriped Italian suit with a crisp white shirt, a gold stick pin across his club tie, diamond cufflinks, and black wingtip shoes. He strode into the meeting room as if he were walking onstage and proceeded to demonstrate one of his company's state-of-the-art products in a way that was irresistible to any human being. He was like a model on *The Price Is Right*, never touching the product except to press a single button. His perfectly memorized script was timed down to the last second, when he gestured toward the output tray and the copies, like magic, appeared.

After a coffee break of almost complete silence, my fellow trainees and I re-entered the room. The trainer took off his jacket and cufflinks, rolled up his sleeves, and proceeded to show us every single weakness and imperfection that machine had—the part the clients never saw. He shattered the myth and banished our fear of the big name. I never bought the hype again and never failed to check out the competition for myself.

The Competitor's Product

And what better way of checking out the competition than using it? It won't work for large-scale products and extensive consulting services, of course, but it's a great idea for tangible goods.

When I moved to Xerox's Toronto office, one of the first things I did was to remove our copier from the mailroom and replace it with a competitor's unit. As I once had been, the salespeople were in awe of the big brand name, but after I forced them to use this machine day in and day out for a couple of months, they realized what a piece of junk it was. The worst thing was having to get down on the floor and use wooden prongs to pull out jammed and scorched paper. Picture it: professionals, in their skirts or suits, clearing this copier on their hands and knees. The next time they went on a sales call and pointed out how easy it was to clear the jams from our copiers, they did it with conviction.

Keep in mind my earlier advice, though—mudslingers fail. You're just trying to gain an appreciation of functional and quality differences so that you can point out the areas in which *your* product excels.

Alliance Partners

We're going to talk more about alliance partners later in the book, but if your company has an ongoing relationship with another firm as a value-added reseller or supplier, it's worth talking to its salespeople, technicians, and even customers for competitive information: What other vendors have you looked at? Why did you choose product Y over product X? Someone has probably already asked these partners the questions you need answered, and a little digging can really pay off. Another place to look: Smart companies have their marketing departments follow up on big sales to add some heft to their brochures and case studies, and they hear a lot more than they use. If you can make a connection with a friendly person in marketing, she might be willing to share good stuff that will later become part of your initial product pitch.

The Internet

For younger sales reps, the Internet is probably the first source for both professional and personal information. But you have to make sure it's not the only stop. Don't get me wrong—with Google and other search engines, you can sometimes find things that even a decade ago you could never have uncovered. But anybody can say anything on the Internet, and that much unfiltered information has two potential flaws: relevance and reliability.

First, relevance. Type in a typical competitor's name and just one of its products, and you could end up retrieving thousands of hits. Even if you're search savvy and use limiters to narrow down the results, you're still likely to retrieve hundreds. Do you really have the time to sift through the fluff to find the useful nugget?

Then there's reliability. How do you know that you're not getting intelligence that's out-of-date or just plain wrong—or, worse, maliciously planted? This is a particular danger on message boards such as those found on Usenet (groups.google.com) and public forums like weblogs (more commonly known as blogs). There are some very specialized groups out there from which you can gain a quick understanding of a certain industry or product, but unless you can find multiple, independent sources for everything you learn, it might be best not to act on it.

All that said, you can at least use a company's official site to see how it's presenting itself and what it trumpets as its strengths; many also make case studies available for download. The business site Hoover's Online (www.hoovers.com) offers capsule reviews of companies' main business and finances; this can be handy for an initial search on both competitors and customers.

Trade Publications

Just about every industry is covered by at least one magazine or newsletter, and some have multiple publications. Flipping through new issues as they come in might yield some useful information, but most of what you'll see is product announcements and personnel changes, not solid details about product or service performance.

In general, I think keeping up with the trade press is slightly more important in the consulting field, but even there a salesperson doesn't have to make an extensive effort. The partners at one of my old firms used to say, "If you don't spend three hours every night reading, you're never going to keep up with what's going on in the IT industry." That was true enough for them—their next call might be to the CIO of Time Warner, to whom they would have to bring something fresh every time they spoke—but I needed only to stay abreast of industry highlights to do my job of getting them in the customer's door.

Now, let's use the competitive edge we've gained to determine the best vertical market for our wares.

Chapter Checklist

To identify and honestly assess your competitors, you have to:

☐ Remember that you will *always* have competition.

☐ Draw up a feature list comparing your product with that of your top three competitors.

☐ Use that list to identify your product's five greatest strengths.

☐ Listen to existing customers who have chosen your product over another vendor's—they can teach you everything you need to know about the differences.

☐ Use other sources of information when necessary: competitors' former employees, a competitor's product itself, your alliance partners, and the Internet (but don't believe everything you read online).

The Third Fundamental: Identifying Your Vertical Market and Assembling Your Tactical Team

The third component of preparing for a million-dollar sale is figuring out the market niche in which your product or service is most likely to succeed. In this chapter, we'll examine ways to test new verticals, which I define below, and discuss the importance of selecting the right competitive tier for your product. We'll also talk about developing what I like to call the "30-second commercial"—a sales rep's primary calling card—as well as some strategies for putting together a small team of technical, service, and support personnel on whom you will rely heavily once you start working at full speed.

Before the concept of vertical markets emerged, all selling was geographic. No matter what your product, you were given a territory and told to knock on every door you passed. But by the early 1980s, it dawned on the sales world that one law office, for example, had basically the same kinds of needs as another law office. One hospital had the same kinds of needs as another hospital—but those needs were different from those of a law firm. Sales gurus realized that training a rep to sell a set of products or applications most relevant to a particular market segment would enable her to gain a valuable edge much more quickly and look that much smarter to new clients. Reps walked in with a measure of credibility, even at their first meeting, because they could lead off with the names of other local hospitals or law firms that had bought their wares.

Vertical markets continued to evolve, and since the 1990s tech boom they've become even more narrowly defined: Now it's not only software for law firms, but software for billing and e-procurement in law firms. Working in a market with such highly differentiated niches can be a problem if you don't have a clear idea of where your product or service fits in—but if you know exactly what your product does and which clients you need to target, you'll drastically cut down on dead-end leads and make up in speed what you lose in breadth.

Starting from Scratch

Many of the people reading this book probably work for established companies that have already identified their verticals and instituted specific strategies. Though I encourage reps in that situation to review the following material anyway—we must constantly reevaluate every aspect of our business if we want to improve—I'm going to concentrate on start-ups and firms expanding into new markets.

When you're just starting out, the foremost things to be concerned with are understanding how your potential clients' industry works and learning the lingo. I'll use the medical-product industry as an example. What is the difference between a pharmaceutical company and a life sciences company? Pharmas comprise a specific niche dealing with the development, manufacturing, and distribution of medicines. Life sciences companies, on the other hand, produce a broader range of medical and biological products. Their focuses are accordingly different, but both are going to have heavy regulatory contact. Both are in constant negotiation with the insurance industry over their pricing. And the list of both differences and similarities goes on. These are the issues you need to have a basic understanding of before you can properly tailor your products to the market.

Within a particular industry, you also need to consider the corporate divisions and department in which your product will play best—will it be procurement, administration, research and development, sales and marketing, or inventory? In my experience, the biggest sales come in areas that have direct bearing on the client's strategic direction: Cutting costs might be important for them, but getting to market faster with a better product is really the holy grail.

Trade publications and the Internet will bring you up to speed on the basics of a particular industry, of course, but your first step should be polling your office to see whether anyone has previous experience in the vertical under consideration. Always use your inside resources to their fullest before going the slower research route. In that vein, reaching out to different divisions within current accounts is another fantastic way to test a new vertical.

Let's say a pharmaceutical company that has been using your product has a growing financial arm. Set up a lunch with your contact and his financial-side colleague—not to sell, but just to brainstorm possible uses for the product. Of course it's great if all the talk gets the financial division excited, but what you're really after is insight into their needs that can be applied to the financial market as a whole.

If you don't have any "friendlies" who can help you with introductions, I suggest that you make appointments with two or three small accounts in the new vertical. Sure, you're going to make mistakes and get banged around a bit, but it will be worth it as long as you're taking notes to improve the presentation. During my time with the consulting firm AnswerThink, we actually did this in the manufacturing sector, and it helped us develop a much better talk track.

After doing some homework on the Web, I called up John Rush (name has been changed), the vice president of a Pittsburgh-based firm that builds sports stadiums, and made an appointment to discuss our supply-chain technology. The supply-chain director and I delivered a corporate PowerPoint presentation highlighting our successes in the pharmaceutical industry, and then put a few suggestions on the table based on our limited understanding of manufacturing. Members of the team John had invited to sit in immediately began to grill us, and they didn't let up. At the end of a fairly uncomfortable two hours, John looked at us sadly.

"I'm sorry, Pat, but it's pretty clear to me that you don't have a good enough grasp of our market for me to take a chance on your company."

We had gone in knowing our chances were slim, and that sealed it. However, the detailed information we gained about supply-chain requirements in the manufacturing sector enabled us to customize the presentation and win business in manufacturing accounts down the road.

Another possible outcome, of course, is that you realize you're never going to get work in a particular vertical. My firm, with extensive experience in building e-procurement systems for corporations, pitched one to Carnegie Mellon University. We had never done one for a university or any other kind of educational client, but we figured that one size fits all. How cocky of us. We found out in short order that there were a number of companies that specialized in e-procurement systems for universities, and one of them got the contract. Rightly so—they could talk the language ten times better than we could, and would have the system up and running much faster. Our competitors already had it built, knew how to execute it, and gave tremendous added value by already having the contacts at various suppliers. We learned a lot from that experience, but after considering the profit margin in the education market, we decided to focus elsewhere. (It's a similar situation with all levels of government, municipal to federal.)

Finding Your Tier

Just as crucial as selecting the right vertical is realistically assessing what business tier you can succeed in. Firms that target solely the Fortune 1000 or even Fortune 500 companies have larger staffs and more robust administrative infrastructure to deal with their clients' high demands; more than likely, you're going to have to grow to that point.

Remember, though, that there are enough middle-tier companies in the world to allow for tens of millions of dollars in sales every year. Continue to increase your core business by fully penetrating the middle-tier market, because dominating a niche can be just as profitable—maybe more—than being a smaller top-tier player. Be realistic about what your company can achieve, but keep trying to make calculated moves into the next tier. Keep knocking on the bigger door because the revenue potential is enormous.

If your company is at the happy point where larger clients are starting to take you seriously, don't fall into the trap of being too rigid about cutoffs. One of my former employers, for example, wouldn't even consider a project under $500,000. One time I went in to meet Andrea Watkins (name has been changed) at Glaxo about a huge security project we had cooked up. That didn't go anywhere—"Who would trust a brand-new vendor with such essential requirements?" she said, correctly—but while we were chatting it came up that she needed a specific programming problem solved, and we had the perfect guy on staff to do it. After seeing his résumé, Andrea signed on right away, and I knew this could be the first step of a profitable long-term relationship.

Trouble was, my boss didn't like that this programming whiz would be tied up on a $50,000 project. "It keeps him from working on the bigger deals," he told me emphatically. It took me 25 minutes to convince him that we needed this small job to earn the right to do business at one of the largest pharmaceutical companies in the world. Once I finally got his approval, we did fabulous work that exceeded the client's expectations, and it did bring us more work with Glaxo.

On the other hand, never jump at a project just for the revenue if you have any doubts about your ability to hit a home run. Even if a customer thinks your solution is a great idea and has the budget, you'd better step back if a close look at the specifics leads you to think you're not going to succeed. It's a tough pill to swallow, but you'll be more respected for knowing your limits than for failing on a big job.

Before we move on to the next chapter, where we'll use the information you've just developed to search for leads, we need to cover two pieces of important back-office work that you'll rely on every day while you're hunting down million-dollar deals.

Creating Your 30-Second Commercial

With the three basic elements of successful sales firmly in your mind—your product, your competition, and your vertical—it's time to create your 30-second commercial. This set speech is the first thing most people will ever have heard about you and your company. Whether for initial telephone contact or networking, it has to convey, in an informative and memorable way, who you are and what benefits you bring.

The elements are pretty simple: Start off with a brief introduction of yourself, your company, and what you do. Your second and third sentences should introduce the business solution you're offering and a proof source (companies that have successfully employed your services). If you already have solid metrics for your product or service—"We were able to increase Company Y's revenue by 49 percent in five weeks"—by all means use them; just be ready with additional proof sources if you're fortunate enough to be talking directly to your prospect and not her voice mail. The closing should be an open-ended but firm request for a time and date to meet.

Here's an actual 30-second commercial I used during my IT sales days:

"Hi, this is Pat Gardner. I'm a sales representative with Brightstation. We recently installed our knowledge management software at Thomson Corp., increasing the accuracy of their information retrieval by 35 percent. The software paid for itself in 90 days. We'd like to come in and speak with you about helping your company increase its productivity. When is a good day for us to get together?"

You can use the same approach with hardware or other durable products:

"Hi, this is Pat Gardner with Phone Anywhere. Our satellite long-distance network saves our customers more than 20 percent a month over their previous telecommunications provider, and they tell us that our installation pays for itself in 9.5 months. Can we meet this Thursday at 10 to discuss giving you the same kind of results?"

When I work up a new commercial, I start by writing it down, trying to be a word minimalist—using the fewest yet most definitive words for what I'm trying to get across. The content has to be specific—"Our knowledge management software allows you to automatically manipulate the millions of pieces of data that come into your company every day"—but must also paint a picture of a business solution that you have in mind for them.

Leave out words such as *innovative* and *revolutionary*, which have become meaningless through overuse. Avoid saying that there are no other products like yours on the market—it makes you sound like a carnival barker and gives the impression that you're going to be boorish and obnoxious to work with. Make sure your pitch doesn't sound too good to be true; too much fluff is guaranteed to fail. And you don't know how many times I've heard "We've got the best people. We do the best work." Take it from me—everybody on the planet says that.

When you're satisfied with the words and have practiced the delivery a few times, I suggest that you run it by members of your family and some friends. Call them up, give them the pitch, and then call again the next day to ask if they can repeat the highlights to you. If you keep getting bouts of silence from the other end of the line, it's time to get out the red pen again. But if they can accurately repeat the high points, try it out next on your sales colleagues or your manager. After last-minute tweaks, you should have a compelling and bulletproof 30-second commercial.

Assembling an Internal Tactical Team

This is where the meetings you conducted during your first few weeks of product training will really reap rewards. It's time to go back to the contacts you made and decide who among them will make strong tactical team members.

Your team will serve many purposes: It will provide experts who can accompany you on sales calls to back up your sketchy knowledge of technical or support specifics, create top-notch proposals while you work on new business, and actually perform the work once the contract is signed. As you did in Chapter 1 when you began your self-training, you might have to reach out to management to explain why you need to create a dedicated team. The benefits, however, are readily apparent.

First we'll discuss finding team members when you're selling equipment or some other durable good, such as furniture or components used in manufacturing. Here we're really talking about a service representative who would be willing to go along to potentially big accounts to talk about your product's reliability. It's likely your choices will be limited to certain people in specific geographical areas, which means cultivating multiple sources in different territories. Look for people who notice when things change or are being built—they see your customers more often than you do, and this kind of attentiveness can produce a great number of leads.

When you're selling tech products or consulting services, you'll probably be able to draw from a wider pool of talent. Especially if you're selling a highly specialized product, you might be tempted to encourage the company's top expert in that discipline to join your team, but keep in mind that the ideal tactical team member probably will not be the most technically adept in the department. People with unusual gifts in one specific area of technology tend not to have the big-picture vision that will best support your selling efforts. Try to identify someone who has broad knowledge about your company's capabilities and knows when a situation requires bringing in a specialist. Often, midcareer techs who are tiring of design or coding and want a new challenge fit the bill perfectly.

After you've brought on the tech or service pillar of the team, it's time to look for someone ready to adopt a fairly new role in high-end sales—the presales team member. Presales bridges the gap between sales and the tech or service side, acting much like a project manager before the close. Likely candidates can often be found among younger techs and junior salespeople who want to change their focus after a few years on the job. Look for someone with great writing and communications skills—presales will not only do background research and write the proposals, but during big meetings will often run the PowerPoint presentation so that the sales rep can observe the audience, expand on certain points, and ask open-ended questions when they can make the biggest impression.

Companies are sometimes reluctant to create presales positions, but it's possible for one presales person to work with two or even three reps at a time, increasing the selling productivity of each one. If a rep is able to complete just one more million-dollar deal per year because presales is handling the back end, the position has paid for itself many times over. Presales is also an excellent conduit for information between the traveling sales staff and deskbound management, improving office communication.

Since your tech person and presales person will be working together a lot when you're not around, it's important that their personalities mesh. It's also imperative that you take prospective team members along on a couple of midlevel meetings to see how they react. Sometimes, as I've found out, just one is more than enough.

One time I was meeting two executives for lunch and took along a tech rep I hadn't previously worked with. Before the lunch I spent 20 minutes going over the call with him, laying out my strategy and instructing him when to stay out and when to jump in. As soon as we sat down and the executives gave us a quick sketch of their needs, he got nervous and never shut up for the rest of the lunch. Instead of listening to them, he changed the whole direction of the meeting by taking 15 minutes to tell them how much their problem sounded like something he'd done for another company. At the end, they thanked us and left. We didn't get the business, and I knew one guy who wasn't going to be on my team.

No matter what you're selling, try to partner with team members who show passion for their jobs, who demonstrate a sense of urgency about deadlines and customer relations, people whose word is their bond. They are the ones who will free you up to do the best selling you can while helping the company deliver the best service to clients. In return, you'll be offering them a chance to be intimately involved with the fastest-moving department in the company, with a large measure of independent responsibility and a chance to move their careers in a new direction.

Now it's time for the last bit of background you need before approaching Codebreakers: finding leads for potential customers.

Chapter Checklist

To identify and enlarge your vertical market, you have to:

☐ Learn the lingo of the industry you're targeting.

☐ Find out which client divisions have the budget for large-scale projects.

☐ Use existing customers to gain an introduction to other departments in the company.

☐ Assess your company's direction and potential—should you try to dominate the middle tier or keep pushing up into the big leagues?

To create a winning 30-second commercial, you have to:

☐ Tell the story of your product in a few sentences—make every word count.

☐ Find a compelling metric from a previous customer's project that demonstrates your product's ROI in terms of time and money saved.

☐ Practice the commercial repeatedly until it's so polished that everyone who hears it can remember the details days later.

To assemble your tactical team, you have to:

☐ Seek out colleagues who understand the technical aspects of your product or service *and* can explain them in layman's terms.

☐ Encourage your sales manager to create a presales position that will handle back-end work while you concentrate on meeting new clients.

☐ Take potential team members on a couple of test calls before you commit.

The Fourth Fundamental: Finding Leads

With the rest of our preliminary work completed, we're now going to wrap up our strategic refresher course with a quick discussion of developing and prioritizing leads for new clients. And when I say leads, I really mean two things: names of people who have budgetary power, of course, but also people who have current, specific business problems that need to be solved. A name by itself isn't nearly as useful as a name that's already attached to an active project.

Too many sales reps look no further than their Rolodexes when they need to uncover fresh leads. I will show you ways to tap into a hundred Rolodexes at once with relatively little effort, and how to keep those leads coming in with some well-timed generosity.

Once you've settled on your particular vertical, the first thing to do is check in with your competition. Go back to the information you developed in Chapter 2, paying special attention to their established client bases. Those lists your competitors helpfully place on their Web sites will tell you which prospects to skip for now. Don't waste your time going after accounts that have already spent big money with someone else in your specialty area—but do keep them on your long-term list and keep your ears open for word that one of them has become unhappy with its current vendors.

(Looked at another way, those lists can also tell you whom to approach right away. If there's a well-known company that none of your immediate competition lists on their sites, it probably means no one has managed to penetrate it, and your product might be just what it's looking for.)

The next avenue to explore is existing alliances and partner-ships, which are crucial if you're going into a vertical market for the first time, because you need to be able to talk to some people to be brought up to speed. Remember, what we're trying to accomplish with this book is learning not only how to be brought up to speed properly, but quickly as well—and what's more efficient than using the resources you have at hand?

When I first entered the pharmaceutical market, I sought out various hardware and software reps from our partner firms who were closing pharma business, asking them about the elements that made them successful in that segment and which key areas they recommended I look into. In the beginning it wasn't about spe-cific leads, just the shape of the market. They taught me about the business applications of the pharma industry, such as the FDA approval process and the resources necessary for new drug research—this is where the big money is.

Later, after I had taken these insights into the field, I was hav-ing a tough time penetrating Johnson & Johnson, the pharma pow-erhouse. I realized that I was working for such a small company that I would continue having problems getting in. Now it was time to go beyond the information-sharing stage with one of my company's existing alliance partners.

Because I had heard around the office that J&J had a lot of Sun Microsystems hardware, I decided to call a former colleague who was now Sun's J&J sales representative. I reached him, explained that I was selling consulting services, and proposed an arrange-ment that became profitable for both of us.

Once you've worked your way through partner contacts, move on to the next level of "friendlies"—satisfied customers who might have a working relationship in the area you're targeting. It'll take some asking around, especially if you're new to the company, but you will probably have completed a lot of that groundwork during your Chapter 1 boot camp. Remember, it's much less threatening when an existing customer introduces you to a potential client. Basically, you're asking him to say, "Would you give X a half-hour of your time? She's been great supporting us. We think she's got a great business solution, and I'm just suggesting that you meet with her to talk about how her product could work in your market."

This is something I did with Unisys when I wanted to break into pharmaceuticals. I realized that the company was doing a tremendous amount of business with Eli Lily, one of the major companies in this area, and my contacts opened doors for me. And not only that—when the success Unisys was having prompted the company to create a pharmaceutical vertical within its own shop, I was introduced to the president of this new division and was able to negotiate an alliance using my software. You're beginning to see the kind of three-dimensional thinking you need to develop when you're working on million-dollar deals.

Tapping a Really Big Rolodex

Once you've made use of your company's business partners and clients, it's time to reach out to your company's staff itself—think of it as spinning through every Rolodex in the building at once. A consulting client of mine employed this tactic with great effect: We sent out an internal, companywide e-mail just asking whether anyone knew someone who worked in the pharmaceutical industry—friend, family member, next-door neighbor, whatever. We got a solid response overall, and really hit pay dirt with one of the back-office employees, whose wife, it turned out, worked as an administrative person at a major pharma company. She gave us five top-notch director-level contacts at the company, names no Internet search would ever have uncovered.

Admittedly, this jackpot was unusual, but it's rare that such a request doesn't turn up at least something usable because colleagues always have multiple avenues of information. Just add up the number of organizations you and perhaps your children belong to—sports leagues, community and professional associations, fraternal groups—and multiply it by the number of people in your company and your circle of friends. It's a huge web of potential contacts, and tapping into it takes surprisingly little time.

I also believe in rewarding someone in my company for providing good information—taking somebody to lunch or giving him a gift certificate to take his spouse to dinner, as we did in this case. We didn't announce a bounty in the e-mail, but showed our appreciation quietly. This kind of unheralded generosity will get around and encourage people to support you, even though you're asking them something that's not in their job descriptions. The good feedback about your generosity could even make it to the future contacts themselves. It doesn't even matter to me whether the leads develop into anything—sponsoring information sharing, from the CEO's office down to the delivery staff, can only benefit the company. One day you'll hit pay dirt with one great contact name.

Networking Properly

Less reliable than the other methods I've detailed but still worthwhile is the networking meeting—if you do it the right way. It pains me to say it, but most people can't network worth a hoot. I can't tell you how many networking meetings I've gone to where people never even attempted to work the room. Often it was more like a drinking club than a valuable business opportunity—some people even brought dates!

Networking is really a ritualized exchange of information. Genuine warmth and interest help you earn the other person's trust, of course, but the true goal is to introduce yourself and your product, receive the same information from your counterpart, and determine whether you can offer any help to each other.

Let me take you along to a typical networking get-together. As soon as I walk into the room, I immediately pick someone nearby, offer my hand, and start in: "Hi, I'm Pat Gardner with Maximum Sales. I help companies increase their revenue by 15 percent within 120 days. And you are?" At this point, your conversation partner should respond in kind: "I'm Jack Samuels with Franklin International. We help companies refinance their short-term debt and improve their financial outlook." Most of the time, though, he won't be so forthcoming, so I'll have to prompt him: "And what do you do, Jack?"

Once I've heard his pitch, the ball is back in my court: "How can I support you in what you do?"

"I'm looking for companies that need portfolio management in the next three months."

"I know my company doesn't need that kind of help right now, but you might want to talk to Jill Brock at Venus Corp. She's right over there. Does Franklin's sales force have any training needs right now?"

"The sales staff is pretty young. There might be an opportunity there."

"Great. Can we talk Thursday at 3:00? Here's my card. It was a pleasure meeting you. If you'll excuse me, my goal today is to meet everyone in the room, and I hope you get a chance to talk with everyone as well."

If you walk into a get-together with your 30-second commercial down perfectly (and the other person is equally concise, of course), the whole process should take about three minutes. If there's interest on either side, make a concrete suggestion for a telephone conversation within a few days, thank him for his time, and move onto the next person.

It's important to learn that networking is not about just getting what you want out of someone else. If you operate with that attitude, you'll fail every time. Even if you make a connection that seems perfect, you have no idea whether even better opportunities await somewhere else in the room—and monopolizing the other person's time will cost him opportunities as well, possibly souring the good contact you've just made.

Prioritizing Your Leads

Once you've finished your exploratory research and calls, and assuming that you don't have a prescribed target list from your sales manager, it's time to figure out where to focus your efforts. From the big pile of leads you've acquired, I suggest coming up with a working list of perhaps 15 accounts, and from there refining it to a top five to go after immediately.

You're going to be weighing quite a few factors: There might be two small companies that appear the easiest to get into because you already know someone working with them currently, and three others that are much bigger prizes but are naturally going to be much harder to sell to successfully. So where to go? Generally, I suggest going for the low-hanging ones first, even if they're not going to be that remunerative, because they'll allow you to build up a reputation rapidly— they will help you earn the right to do business at larger accounts.

I'm always looking to get in at least at the "C level"—that is, Chief Executive Officer, Chief Financial Officer, Chief Information

Officer, or chief of a division. These executives deal with the critical business questions that decide how well a company is going to do in the next two to three years. They have the power and the money to identify problems and implement solutions. They are at the center of the most exciting opportunities in the business world.

Going in at a high level can make a huge difference. For example, you might have good information that your product would fit in exactly with a particular project—it would seem to make sense, then, to go straight to the project manager. But maybe not: It might turn out that that project manager is only overseeing the prototype, and someone else is tackling the full implementation three months from now. Unless you're getting in at the C level, where the exec has an exact sense of every project that's going to be crucial to his area's success in the next 12 months, you might do a $100,000 deal only to miss a million-dollar one.

When you're breaking into a new account, you're going to end up talking to two different high-level prospects: decision makers and influencers. The decision makers are vice presidents or division chiefs who are ultimately responsible for approving projects and budgets; they're the ones you want to see but don't always get to see. The influencers are the people, usually more technically oriented, who are really going to test your product, ask the really important questions, and make the decision on whether your product or service will tie into their goals and work as advertised.

Many times, though, you're going to get leads from a lower level than you're shooting for, but that doesn't mean they aren't useful. One obvious thing to do is to call them up and ask if they can direct you to the right person. One of the best contacts of my career was an administrative assistant at a huge firm. Presidents and vice presidents of the different divisions I used to sell to came and went all the time, but she was there for 20 years. Coming back to that account after a five-year absence I could call her up and say, "Let's go out to lunch and talk." She would tell me who was handling what, who was new, who the power brokers were, who the influencers were, and who the decision makers were. A lot of salespeople think, "A secretary isn't worth my time," but as a presidential-level assistant, this woman was the hub of what was happening.

People who have an inside edge at the account are an essential resource. Think of how helpful it is to know personnel and political situations—wouldn't you love to hear "The person on this project is the director of such and such, but he's leaving in 30 days, and he's being replaced by this person, so you might want to see both" or "They're never going to approve his budget because this person blew it last year with two other projects that failed." Everyone is worthy of your respect and your time, especially those who might be there long after people in higher positions have moved on.

With your strategic sales skills refreshed, your top targets set, and the names of some high-level contacts on your to-do list, you're probably raring to sell. Even if you stop reading at this point, you're better equipped to make big deals than many of your competitors, because you've begun to think cooperatively and three-dimensionally. But you should resist the urge to rush out and go it alone because we're now moving to the core concept of the book and the real secret of finding and closing those huge deals—the Codebreaker.

Chapter Checklist

To ferret out and prioritize promising sales leads in a new vertical, you have to:

- ☐ Analyze your competitors' client lists to see who's bought recently—and who isn't buying.

- ☐ Check in with alliance partners for market information and specific opportunities.

- ☐ Ask satisfied customers to introduce you to their colleagues.

- ☐ Put out an internal companywide call for potential contacts—and reward that information.

- ☐ Use networking meetings to your greatest advantage by perfecting the three-minute information-sharing ritual.

- ☐ Take smaller clients seriously if they present immediate opportunities—a successful project is your best advertisement.

- ☐ Aim for the C level—chiefs are the executives with the money and power to solve business problems—but use any lower-level contacts you develop to their fullest.

The Codebreaker

Finding Your Codebreakers

Despite increasing academic analysis of salesmanship and sales systems, despite increasing management sophistication, despite technological advances that allow workers to trade relevant information in ever faster and more varied ways, a newly hired sales rep at a typical company will still hear almost exactly this on her first day: "Here's your territory, here's a list of prospects, and here's your quota. You've got 12 months to achieve it."

Even if you've been hired because you have a Rolodex full of great contacts in a certain market segment, your new colleagues are probably already servicing some of those accounts—you're almost guaranteed to be starting from scratch with at least a few new prospects.

You know what this feels like. When a rep has no prior experience with an account, when he's starting at the receptionist's desk like anyone else, it can take three to six months to uncover names and develop the relationships that will get him to a high-level decision maker. Multiply that by 3 or 5 or 10, and you've got a lot of hard rowing to meet the quota.

You already know that I don't think too highly of this sink-or-swim system, but until the benefits of team-oriented sales management strategies become more well known, we're pretty much stuck with it. So how can a rep leapfrog over the lower levels of a potential customer's hierarchy—and all of her competition—to get to those high-level decision makers in half the time or less, while both exceeding quota and acting as a test case for the multiple advantages of cooperation in sales? The answer is a select class of professionals that I call *Codebreakers*.

A Codebreaker, put simply, is someone who has demonstrated his or her worth to a client a hundred times over and accordingly represents a direct connection to director- or executive-level contacts who have problems to solve and a budget to spend on them. As we'll see in this chapter, Codebreakers come in all shapes and sizes—they can be measured by the amount of yearly business they're writing with a particular client, or the mission-critical importance of the work they're doing—but they're certainly not just sitting behind a desk waiting to be found. In my experience, the metrics of Codebreakers break down like this: Research and call 20, meet with 9, work with 3.

Using some of the same techniques you employed to narrow your list of prospects in Chapter 4, you will try to identify multiple Codebreakers with whom you can partner to hit your targets quickly, efficiently, and profitably.

The Types of Codebreakers

There are really three kinds of Codebreakers—external, internal, and customer. Externals are the big prize—as with most things, the harder they are to find, the greater the reward for doing so—but all three have a place in your strategy. Let's go over the types briefly before getting into the details.

External

This type, the classic Codebreaker, is a sales rep from a noncompeting company who is writing millions of dollars' worth of business with an account you're trying to penetrate. These hard-working, ego-driven individuals have become established, trusted vendors by creating and repeatedly proving value to the client. When, for example, an HP rep is selling $40 million of equipment and services a year to Johnson & Johnson, you know he's an integral vendor from an operations standpoint—he helps keeps the lights on, sometimes literally. When these people knock on the door, the client shows them right in.

A subtype of the external Codebreaker is someone who might not be doing large amounts of business on a regular basis but who recently crafted the perfect solution to a complex problem that was costing the client millions in lost revenue. This person, I assure you, will have a free pass to the executive level for some time to come.

With an external Codebreaker, the goal is a partnership that aligns his product or service and one of yours in a way that's compelling to the client. After getting in, you pull out all the stops to prove your value and use that success as a springboard for ongoing big deals, either with the Codebreaker or on your own. What's his reward? Increased sales and value for his current clients, and the chance to crack the top levels at your big accounts.

Internal

Internal Codebreakers are fellow reps at your company who either sell a different product or service, or sell the same line as you in a different territory. If your company's sales team is organized along the right lines, internal Codebreakers are probably the easiest to get—I'm sure you don't need me to tell you how to radiate within an established account—but don't underestimate how valuable a colleague might be when you're trying to attract an external Codebreaker. What if the reciprocal accounts you have to offer don't interest him, but you find out he's been desperate to pitch a company that is one of the biggest clients of the guy in the next

office? (Here you start to get a hint of the three-dimensional thinking that's crucial to using Codebreakers successfully.)

Customer

When you can get one, it's great to have a customer Codebreaker—
a satisfied client who has a strong relationship with an executive at
a noncompeting company and who's willing to make a personal
case for how valuable your solutions have been. It's true that the
stars don't often align in this pattern, but it's the perfect incentive to
learn more about your clients and their industry position.

Finding Codebreakers

Unless you're employed by a huge company with a widely scattered
sales force, internal and customer Codebreakers are relatively
easy to find—you just have to check in regularly with your colleagues to see what they've closed (which you hope also leads you
to a satisfied client) and what they're shooting for next. External
Codebreakers represent the real challenge: Every contact you
make has the potential to bring you one step closer to a
Codebreaker, or even to *be* a Codebreaker, but it's going to take a
lot of detective work to make the necessary connections.

Start this search off right by mastering one simple technique:
Every time you find yourself talking to someone new at a customer or a vendor, use open-ended conversation starters: "Tell me
more about your business. Tell me a little about what you do." At
a comfortable point during the answer, ask, "Oh, and who are you
working with?"

You've already gotten them talking; everything's friendly and
relaxed. Typically, this is the kind of response you'll get: "I'm working with Microsoft, and we do some of our security work at Exide."

And now you move lightly but firmly to get your information: "You know, I was thinking about calling Exide about a different project. Would you mind giving me the name and phone number of your sales rep?" If you sense a little hesitation, you might even want to describe the project generically, so that the contact doesn't think you're trying to poach his firm's work. Ultimately, if you use this approach without fail, you will quickly build up a strong list of potential Codebreakers.

So where to begin? In addition to the leveraging of internal contacts that you learned earlier in the book, there are a few other relatively direct methods of prospecting for names. Flipping through the sign-in log while you're waiting in the reception area is one of the oldest tricks around—who's been making multiple calls at the same division over the last few months? For example, one time I was in the lobby of a very large pharmaceutical company, waiting for my appointment with a midlevel contact, when I met the HP sales rep, who was signing in ahead of me. I introduced myself by saying, "I see your name in this book as much as mine. I'm Pat Gardner from ABC Consulting Group. I've read that you're providing equipment for this company's new client database. We do a lot of consulting work in that area. Why don't you and I talk about how we could grow revenue together?"

With the increased emphasis on security, and with signing in inevitably becoming an electronic process, you might have to step lightly, but if you find a paper logbook and a receptionist who's willing, you can get a quick picture of your target's important vendors (and, incidentally, your competition).

As we also saw in the first section of the book, Web sites can be a gold mine of quick information about your competition. But because many sites also list their alliance partners along with their customers, if you can identify even one partner you know would be a great fit with your product or service, you have laid a clear path for yourself to your ultimate target. Again, three-dimensional thinking: There's always a way you can single out the Codebreaker who best matches your core competencies and then persuade her to take you in to a very high level.

If you're really starting from scratch and your internal sources have come up empty, you'll have to cast your net a bit wider. One of the surprising secrets I reveal during every Codebreaker seminar I teach is that the press release archives of client Web sites are brimming with names of executives and vital large-scale projects. This public information source should be your first stop when looking for leads. I found a wonderful Codebreaker by reading a release about a new strategic relationship between GSK and a customer information firm. Seeing the name of the information firm's VP of sales in the release, I called him up and sold him call center support. In turn, I was able to use the success of that project to do further work with GSK.

Next, think of the major players who are almost undoubtedly doing at least some business with your client—service companies such as Waste Management Inc. or Deloitte & Touche, supply houses such as OfficeMax or Hammermill Paper, and also large regional companies. You might already know people who work for these big vendors in some capacity, and you can use these contacts to network your way to a Codebreaker. You're probably going to need multiple lines of inquiry going on because you are going to run into frequent roadblocks. Why? For the same reason you want these folks—they are very busy closing millions of dollars' worth of business.

Though it can be a bit hit or miss, simply calling around to companies whose products you think will match well with yours can also yield results. When you're trying to get inside a Fortune 500 company, you're dealing with a pool of potentially hundreds of vendors who are doing big numbers. You want to think in terms of a good partnership in which you're both going to benefit, and you can achieve this by knowing your product and knowing what your company does.

Another worthwhile avenue to try is calling around the lower levels of the target client itself. While you're making these kinds of inquiries, you're also asking some of those same open-ended questions I mentioned before: "What else does IBM do here? Do you *know* the IBM rep?" It could turn out that they're not just selling equipment—they might be running the entire global outsourcing department and the internal call center. You need this information so that you can approach your Codebreaker knowing more than just one dimension of what that person might be able to do for you.

It might seem a little counterintuitive to ask the client's employee to give you the name of an outside vendor rep—why not just ask him for the name of his division chief? Well, think about it—he doesn't want to be responsible for passing you up the company chain. What if it comes back to haunt him for some reason? But there's little chance of harm in giving you the name of a vendor's salesperson. Passing along that information will get you off the phone and take the matter out of his hands—a big relief on both counts.

You're not yet where you want to be, but you're gaining valuable insight into the culture of both the prospect company and the Codebreaker's firm. When you finally get the Codebreaker on the phone and wow her with your 30-second commercial, the contacts you've made will help to assure her of your credibility: "I was talking to Mary Smith, and she was really impressed by how much your latest project saved her division last quarter. She thought it would be good for us to talk because she saw that there is value in our working together."

It's going to be a lot of work at first, and the connections aren't just going to fall into place, but that's OK. Start small, get knocked around a little bit, and then go after the bigger fish. Remember the mantra: Every call can bring you one step closer.

Evaluating Your Potential Codebreakers

Ultimately, you should be approaching reps who are doing at least $5 million in business a year with your target client. You're not going to be shooting for a $40 million Codebreaker the first time—you're going to have to establish yourself and prove value to a smaller Codebreaker before a heavy hitter is going to give you the time of day.

Of course, it's often more than just the numbers. I put almost as much focus on whether the person is good to partner with. Is he working on some really crucial projects? Sometimes the product or service he's selling isn't particularly expensive, but is essential to the client's short-term goals (the next 12 to 24 months) or is an integral part of its mission. In these cases, the rep might be doing $2 million or $3 million, but in such an important area that it's worth pursuing so that you can support his solution and prove your worth in a critical situation.

I've wasted some lunches meeting with people who turned out not to be doing as much business or as interesting business as they seemed, but these occasional disappointments sharpen your faculties and attune you to the signs that someone isn't Codebreaker material.

Another thing to be aware of is that some Codebreakers could be doing big business at more than one client. I met one rep who was doing $20 million each at two different companies. One of them wasn't on my client list, but it was on the list of one of my colleagues; when I had solidified our relationship, I introduced them to each other, acting as an internal Codebreaker myself.

There are a lot of different levels to the Codebreaker strategy. That's why I talked earlier about the difference between being interested only in your own quota and being a company player, and also looking at where you can increase your own value within your company. If you want to move up the corporate ladder, you'll start growing Codebreakers who benefit your entire firm.

Getting the Crucial First Appointment

You've got names, you've done the background homework—it's time to move forward. This is the first high-stakes moment in the quest for a million-dollar deal. You have to have your 30-second commercial down pat to be able to even approach a Codebreaker because a Codebreaker could actually be as big, if not bigger, than your most important client. Why? Because he might have inside access to two or three of your potential accounts, or know someone who does. Recognize that a Codebreaker is as important as the CEO of a company.

The call itself is pretty straightforward, lasting maybe two minutes at most. Here's a typical script:

- Introduce yourself: "This is Gail Madison with Simons Corp."

- Use the best name you've uncovered in your search: "I understand that your janitorial company is doing a lot of business with Susanne Lee in the facilities management department at Wal-Mart. I've researched your firm, and I'd like to propose an alliance with our product."

- Run through your 30-second commercial: "We've found that customers who use our new concentrated floor cleaning fluid need 47 percent less than when using comparable products on the market today. Based on the square footage of the stores you're servicing, this represents a savings of up to $21,437 per store per year."

- Close: "As you can see, I think our products are perfect for an alliance. Let's talk. Let's meet next Thursday. I'll buy you lunch."

And that's it. It can be a real nail-biter, but if you go in prepared your chances are excellent. Anytime you can introduce someone to a project that will increase his revenue stream, he is going to be interested in talking to you. Your Codebreaker thinks, "I won't have to do that much work to get extra millions of dollars of revenue because I have this partner who's going to be finding the projects and bringing me in."

How does it bring your Codebreaker this extra revenue? Here's an example. When I was selling IT consulting services, I was able to align with one of the largest hardware manufacturers because every piece of its equipment needed consulting services to accompany it. After giving the lowdown on what my company did, my offer to the other rep was essentially this: "If you decide to partner with me and bring me in to your hardware customers, I can introduce you to some places where I'm doing consulting services work and there's often a need for new hardware." He loved it. It's a strategy I've followed over and over again to break into new companies and create repeatable business solutions at others that were worth millions of dollars.

By the way, I always try to make sure my first meeting with a Codebreaker is at lunch because a certain vulnerability is created when people break bread together, and with that vulnerability comes openness. If you show you're open, the other person will almost always do the same, and it takes down a lot of the barriers. Plus it's a great way to sidestep the "I'm too busy" objection—everybody has to eat sometime. If you hear those dreaded words, here's how to handle it: "You know what? I know this restaurant right down the street from your building. I'll meet you there and take just 45 minutes of your time." We'll talk more about the right way to handle this meeting in the next chapter.

Knowing When It Won't Work

There are, of course, plenty of successful salespeople with the contacts and the big revenue who would nevertheless make lousy Codebreakers. In my experience, you have to meet nine to get three you can work with regularly. When you're scouting, how can you tell the difference before getting in too deep?

I've found that the prime indicator is attitude, which will be apparent even in your first conversation. Instead of pressing you about where and when you're going to get him inside access at one of your clients, the true Codebreaker will tell you what he's done for his customers. Codebreakers will be straight with you about the value add, ROI, and differentiator they're bringing to their clients, and they should be able to show you that they understand how your product or service will enhance that.

For example, I once met a rep named Sara Segal (name has been changed) to talk with her about doing security services consulting business with her firm. After I presented my company's proof sources and tried to open the conversation about how we could partner, she proceeded to grill me about what accounts I was working in, who my contacts were, and when we could send our representatives to her training program. She kept pushing me to sign a value-added reseller agreement—a contract that would have obligated me to sell a certain volume of her product annually—at the first meeting! But she wasn't offering anything in return—no ideas for a strategic partnership, no names of other accounts we could approach together; in short, she just wanted me to do her job for her. We didn't have a second conversation.

There are some relatively successful people out there who are more order-takers than really professional sales reps. The order-takers are not going to be able to tell you the importance of their projects or what their product is doing for the client. If you ask the right questions, just as you would when trying to discover the extent of a potential customer's resources, you can figure out pretty quickly whether a particular salesperson will be of value to you.

Even during the first conversation, a good Codebreaker will already be looking for benefits to working with you. Every single opportunity, everybody he meets, everybody he networks with, he's looking for an opportunity to grow revenue. This is how they get to be as good as they are—they're always open to it, and they emphasize the positive rather than the negative. If someone seems obnoxious or high-maintenance, that should throw up a caution flag for you—if you try to partner with him, he's going to drive you crazy.

Now that you've sidestepped any obvious mismatches and made an appointment, let's get to lunch and get that Codebreaker on your team.

Chapter Checklist

To identify and attract Codebreakers, you have to:

☐ Learn the three types—external, internal, and customer—and their relative merits.

☐ Prospect for Codebreaker leads by always asking new business contacts open-ended questions about their work and whom they're working with.

☐ Exercise three-dimensional thinking—with every new piece of information you gather, ask yourself "How can I put this together with what I already know to get myself closer to my target?"

☐ Search press release archives of company Web sites—they're a treasure-house of important projects and high-level contact information.

☐ Identify 20 potential Codebreakers to call through your research, aim to meet with nine of them, and expect to work with three.

☐ Evaluate potential Codebreakers not only by the amount of business they do with your target client, but also by how crucial their application is to the client's bottom line—a $3 million Codebreaker who helps to keep the lights on is a better match than a $10 million order-taker.

☐ Realize that a Codebreaker is as important as a CEO. Prepare your pitch accordingly.

☐ Accept that some potential Codebreakers, no matter how good their numbers, won't grasp the give-and-take nature of a partnership approach.

Working with Codebreakers

We've now identified our immediate client targets and found the names of potential Codebreakers who can help us get in at the highest levels of those accounts. The job now is to convince the Codebreaker that a partnership with you will increase his revenue, improve his standing with his customer, and lead him to new opportunities with some of your clients.

Before we get going on Codebreakers, I want to clear something up. I've found that some people, when first hearing about the Codebreaker concept, think it's not really fair—they're convinced it's a form of riding someone else's coattails to get into an account. But nothing could be further from the truth: A Codebreaker is never going to work with you unless you bring value to her product or improve her position at her company. There could be active projects that you could assist with, or add value to, with your product. Or perhaps the Codebreaker is in phase one of a project but looking ahead to the consultants she'll need in phase three—consultants you know. You want to be there over the long haul with this person. You want to be there when she's starting new projects, just as you want her to be there when you start projects on your own.

With that out of the way, let's look at the prospect list and find some Codebreakers.

The First Phone Call

In most ways, your first call to a Codebreaker is like any other sales call. You're going to use the same tools as you would when making an initial call to a potential client, but you have to be even more succinct with Codebreakers. Prove your value within the first five minutes or you're done. If he's keeping you on the phone longer, it's a good indication of how interested he is.

Before you dial, there are a couple of cautions: Don't make an elaborate introduction, and don't mention having seen something about the person in a magazine or at a seminar unless it is very recent. Drop a name if it's relevant, but unless you've been briefed by a reliable source about a company's internal politics, don't lead with a referral from someone else in the company—it can backfire if that person doesn't like or respect the person you mention. Get to the core of your message without stalling.

In the course of the call, you'll have to touch on these essential elements so that the benefits of partnering with you are clear:

- Exactly how your product or service is going to complement the Codebreaker's offerings

- How your product is going to assist or even improve his current solution for the client

- How it's going to raise his value with his client by showing that he's willing to partner to create better business solutions

- The selling opportunities you can offer him in exchange for his assistance

When he picks up the phone, start the ball rolling with a flawless rendition of your 30-second commercial (highlighting, of course, your differentiator, value add, and ROI) and your two proof sources. Hold another two enticing facts in reserve in case you're not piquing the level of interest you want with your main presentation, or if the Codebreaker is so interested he needs to hear more right away. But don't give him everything. You want to get him excited about meeting with you and have him start thinking about how you'll be working together before you even get together.

If you've created that level of interest, it's fantastic—you've done your job well. But if your prospect starts to stonewall when it comes to making a face-to-face appointment, it's usually for one of three reasons: You haven't shown enough value for him to bother to spend the time; he is literally too busy to see you; or he's been burned in partnerships before.

If you can tell from his voice that he's still willing to hear a little more, this is the time to deploy whatever you've kept in reserve, which should be pure value propositions: "By automating information sharing among divisions, we helped Client Y bring its latest product to market two months ahead of schedule. Together we can do the same thing for your client." It's your last shot, so make it count.

If he's too busy, you've got to show that you understand his situation and are committed to adding value to his product without adding to his workload. I suggest something along these lines: "I'm not going to waste your time with a bunch of meetings. I'm not asking you to sell my product for me. I'm just asking you to make a couple of introductions, and the reason I want to meet with you is to explain my proposition in slightly more detail. I'm not going to show you a PowerPoint presentation or bore you with technical details. If you give me the opportunity to meet with you for lunch, I will share with you where I think the best *solutions* lie, and how we might work together."

If he's reluctant to entertain the idea of any sort of partnership, you can probably guess he's had a really bad relationship at some point. Ask about it gently: "What kind of experience have you had working with alliance partners?"

"I have wasted more time, more energy, and more effort in trying to partner with people," he might say, "and not one of them got me into a single deal."

Now, he may not be that open and honest with you on the phone, but you know that's what he's thinking. You need to make him forget about his bad experiences with a confident response: "I am different from everyone else you've ever partnered with before, because I set time lines, I set goals, I set dates, and I set delivery, in terms of what we're going to do together."

The goal of this call isn't just to close for lunch, of course; through some quick questions and answers, you want to gather as much information as you can about the Codebreaker so that you can work out how to hit the bull's-eye when you get to lunch. Essentially, you're trying to find out two things—where he's been successful, and where his pain is: "I have a great product, but I can't penetrate the customer relationship management market."

Whatever information the Codebreaker shares with you over the phone is what you're going to focus your immediate research on. You have to have a clear-cut understanding of what it was that sparked his interest enough for him to meet you. You could have several things you want to talk about at that initial meeting, but what is it that *he* wants to hear about?

Try to aim for your lunch just a few days in the future—you want to be fresh in his mind, and you want to show that you can get things done quickly with a minimum of fuss. Once you're off the phone, send an e-mail right away that casually confirms the day and time ("I've made reservations at the California Café—see you Tuesday at noon") and give a link to a pertinent piece of information available on your Web site, such as a case study (a short write-up explaining how a previous client successfully employed your product) or client list that shows strength in the area you'll be discussing (but keep it to just a link or two—don't overload it).

Codebreakers are smart, and this gives them the opportunity to look up something about you in anticipation of the meeting. If you're dealing with a true professional, you'll get a response in kind—the good ones do their homework because they're looking for additional revenue out of you.

The First Lunch

This first meeting is very focused with a clear objective, and you want to make it as laid back and fun as possible. How do you do that? Preparation, preparation, preparation. You plan how you're going to start the conversation, what you're going to talk about, and what—if all goes well—will be the result.

While you're researching whatever information leads you gleaned during the phone call, don't neglect to attend to the practical details of the lunch. Scope out the restaurant ahead of time and talk with the maître d'. Let him know you intend to use the restaurant frequently, and that you need an out-of-the-way table and a waiter who's not going to be interrupting you all the time. Make yourself familiar so that when the Codebreaker arrives and gives your name, it looks to him as if you're known there.

The day of the lunch, get there early, say, 12:45 for a 1:00 p.m. meeting, and seat yourself so that you're the one facing out toward the bustle of the room, which ensures that your lunch companion will have to pay attention to you.

When you're actually sitting across from the Codebreaker, start off very, very slowly. Don't run your mouth off about business before he even has a chance to look at the menu; allow a few minutes to build rapport through general chit-chat. Be relaxed, so that you'll be thought of as someone who will be very easy to work with. Think back to some of the first dates you've had—didn't you used to be turned off by people who came on too strong? Codebreakers are busy, stressed people, and you want to put them at ease.

I can't emphasize enough that you should bring as little as possible and you should eat as little as possible. If you're hungry, eat

before you get there. I'm serious. This is *not* about food. I'm not getting spaghetti and wrapping it around my fork—I usually order salad
and take three or four bites. You'd be amazed at how many people
who set up these meetings have three drinks and gorge themselves on huge meals; when you do that, you can't talk or focus on
what's going on. Let the Codebreaker eat, of course—filet mignon
or whatever he wants. Equally important is to leave the white
papers and full-color PowerPoint printouts back at the office.
Nobody wants that stuff handed to him nowadays. He can get it
from your Web site. Don't risk looking like a rookie.

Once you've shown the Codebreaker that you aren't trying to
micromanage the meeting, he'll usually lead the conversation into
the business portion. It's OK to allow him to be in control for part of
the meeting, because they *are* control freaks—in a good way. Your
letting him take the lead tells him that later, when the two of you are
talking to the CEO or CIO of Company X, you're not going to be
fighting with him for the Chief's attention. It's his customer, right?

Once you're given your opening, reinforce what you talked
about on the phone, because he's forgotten. Everybody forgets
what he talked about on the phone more than two days ago.
Mention something about his product and company to show that
you've done your homework and say that you think there's a good
partnership possibility here.

A good Codebreaker is then going to turn to you and want
more detail about that—why do you think you can add value to
someone who's already doing $20 million a year at Wyeth? He is
going to challenge you a little bit, so be ready for it—it happens to
him all the time on his own calls, and he's actually getting a chance
to be the customer for once. As with your 30-second commercial,
be a clear, concise, memorable word minimalist: "Here was the
problem at Company C, and here's what we did to solve it—saving
them 30 percent in three months." Or if he's a little dubious because

you don't have experience in his vertical, say something like "Our expertise has been in manufacturing, but here's why we think our product will play beautifully in your area."

When you get down to the business talk, you should have a "flow chart" strategy in mind: The best outcome is that you agree to do a project together. If not that, then try to persuade the Codebreaker to give you a personal introduction to your target. If not that, maybe the Codebreaker can give you a new name or two, closer to the desired C level, that you can follow up on yourself.

If another source has already given you the name of a likely target, you can run this past the Codebreaker: "I think Bob Smith is the guy I want to see; what do you think about that? Do you know what he does, or what his projects are?" It might turn out that he doesn't know Bob, but does know his colleague Mary Lou. It's a bit like fencing at this point in the conversation—you might be going back and forth a few times, gaining some information but not any real indication whether he wants to partner with you. Remember that your real goal is to earn the right to do business and go with this person to a much higher level. If all you're getting is names, it's time to say, "I thank you for this information, and I'm definitely going to follow up right away and let you know what the results are, but what I really want to discuss is how our products could be put together as a single solution for this client and others."

We've hit the nitty-gritty now. Some potential Codebreakers are just very, very good salespeople who might have inherited a territory, and they might not be able to build an alliance with you because they might not be able to think out of the box enough to figure out how it could be developed. But a really powerful Codebreaker is looking to build—he's closed a $5 million deal and wants to close a $10 million deal. He's always looking for the bigger and better opportunity, and he likes to think creatively. Give him a little space to respond thoughtfully. If you suggest to him how you think you could build an alliance and then let him chew on it, it allows him to come back to you and say, "We *might* be able to do *this*. Tell me more about it." You've just laid the foundation for your alliance.

You might not get a definite answer at lunch; for example, the Codebreaker might have to go back and get his technical people involved or run the alliance idea by his boss. But the top-notch ones, who know everything that's going on at both the sales and corporate levels, might be able to give you the go-ahead right there.

If the Codebreaker seems reluctant to talk about a partnership, there's something wrong. Most likely, you still haven't proven your value. He might just throw you a bone so the lunch isn't a total loss. If this happens, follow it up with "Thank you very much for giving me this name and number, and I will absolutely take the best care of him. I'll be sure to say wonderful things about you, and see if that customer and I can work together." But to be sure, bring it back: "What I really want to do is focus on this with you, and build an alliance. Tell me what you think about that." If he hems and haws, then you might want to say something that's more leading: "Perhaps your company is already working on a similar alliance, or you don't see the value to it." Try to direct it to the specific reason he's objecting. If you can't get a straight, easily understandable answer, try this approach: "I have one person I'd really like to get in to see. Why don't we do that one and see how that goes? If that doesn't work out great for both of us, we'll go our separate ways." As long as you've been able to make some impact, he'll probably do one appointment.

Whichever way it turns out, finish the lunch exactly when you promised and sincerely show your appreciation for his time and interest. Follow up with an e-mail showing that you have all the details under control and move on to whatever you've agreed to do.

Compensating a Codebreaker

Compensation might or might not come up at the first lunch, so it's good to be prepared to discuss it. The best way to compensate a Codebreaker is to increase her business, whether through gaining her additional work at her current clients or introducing her to your clients. That might be all you need: "If you take me to see John Doe, I'll take you to see Bob Smith." Codebreakers who work together create a pipeline and a timeline; if one of the two parties is not doing what she's supposed to do, the whole thing breaks down, so you've got to do it—and fast.

If your Codebreaker isn't interested in that approach—and the best ones always are—you might have to create a revenue arrangement: "If I close a $100,000 deal in 90 days, I'll give you $5000." That's going to get her attention, but unless you can convince your sales manager to set up a formal Codebreaker system that makes these payments, it's going to come out of your pocket.

In some ways, though, it's better not to promise a monetary amount, but some kind of specific gift: "I want you and your spouse to go down to the electronics store and pick out a flat-screen TV." You've already arranged this with someone at a store in their area, and your Codebreaker is taken care of. This way you don't have to put a dollar limit out there on the table—give the TV salesman a limit and let him deal with it. Trips are another great motivator. Certainly these big-time salespeople can afford such things for themselves, but what you're really giving them is an excuse to do it. Taking a vacation on your own dime is never quite as enjoyable as when someone else is footing the bill.

It's true that $5000 is a good chunk of your commission on a $100,000 deal, but it's meant to get you in the door of a multimillion-dollar account. Once you can list that as one of your marquee clients, you'll see it would have been worth 10 TVs to get in there.

Some Codebreakers need these inducements and some don't. Either way, you're going to get the high-level contact you want.

Going It Alone

An important point to keep in mind is that a Codebreaker is no substitute for doing your homework on a potential client. Codebreakers can dramatically speed up the sales process, but if you can't find an appropriate Codebreaker you have to be ready to forge ahead alone, and you don't want to be caught without a clue as to what to do next.

And sometimes it does make sense to try going it alone. As valuable as cultivating Codebreakers is, it does take time and add a layer of complexity to your sales efforts. If you find yourself in the fortunate position of having a solid, high-level contact *and* you're confident about the competitive information you've developed about your target's needs, it makes sense to pursue the lead as soon as it's feasible.

You want to get in this door at this company, into a place where you can talk serious business. That's what to look at: "What accounts do I want to go after? Do I have anybody who can help me get in there? If not, I'll get all my other information on the Internet and I'll just start calling people, or I'll start with the CEO or CIO."

Don't be afraid to call up a C-level person and tell his assistant, "I'm not sure your boss will be interested, but here's what I do." She may give you an in; many times I've been given the name and number of a more appropriate contact. Administrative assistants keep their positions by looking out for the boss's best interests. If you have a compelling story about what you do—"We just sold a million-dollar software project to your competitor ABC Company"—you have a good chance of making it past the gatekeeper.

If you do go in without a Codebreaker and come out empty-handed, it doesn't mean you can't keep trying to develop a Codebreaker who can take you back to the same contact in a stronger position, but it might be a signal to start looking elsewhere in the target company. Ideally, you will always be pursuing two or three or even more angles at the same prospect, so that the minute one avenue dries up you can concentrate your efforts on another one.

Now, whether you've got a Codebreaker at your side or you're braving it alone, it's time to strategize three potential projects to take into the crucial first sales call.

Chapter Checklist

To gain a meeting and partner with a Codebreaker, you have to:

☐ Build the presentation for your first phone call around not only your company's successes, but also the benefits a partnership will bring to the Codebreaker.

☐ Have a secondary set of value propositions and proof sources to fall back on if the Codebreaker's reaction is lukewarm during the call.

☐ Try to close for lunch just a few days after the call so that you remain fresh in the Codebreaker's mind.

☐ Make the lunch as low-key as possible for the Codebreaker—leave the brochures and white papers at the office, and let him take the lead in getting down to business.

☐ Show that you've done your homework by mentioning a few of her company's recent successes, and then ask what areas she could use help in.

☐ Adopt a flowchart strategy to reach your goals for the lunch—aim for an alliance, then work your way through alternatives.

☐ Set definite short-term goals if the partnership looks promising—and hit them.

If you can't find a Codebreaker to take you into an otherwise promising target, you have to:

☐ Be ready to go it alone—call every contact you can uncover in an attempt to connect the dots (and I mean every contact: call the executive's assistant and give him your pitch).

Developing Three Projects and Preparing for the First Sales Call

Once you and your Codebreaker have agreed to work together, your first joint task will be to put your respective tactical teams on alert about the new alliance. There should be a brief and orderly transfer of technical information to each side, perhaps even a formal demonstration meeting if your teams aren't familiar with each other's products. The object of this exchange is to allow you to brainstorm with your respective teams about how your products will best complement each other and how to approach the client you're trying to penetrate. You and the Codebreaker will then review each side's ideas before you start going out on calls.

Your Codebreaker might have some very specific ideas about what to try first at the target client, and at this early point in the relationship you should honor that. However, it doesn't mean you and your team shouldn't be as creative as possible—this is the time to put both obvious and radical ideas out on the table. From among these ideas, you'll pick three projects that are the best marriage of your products' capabilities and the potential client's needs.

Why three projects? You're trying to maximize the opportunity the Codebreaker has given you. You will have gotten in to see someone you might never have been able to reach on your own.

What happens if the first project you propose, the one you're sure is a winner, is shot down in two minutes with a "That's not even on our radar screen" or "We've already got that handled?" If that's the only arrow in your quiver, you've just lost a huge chance. Better to come in with two more ideas—related, perhaps, but targeting different divisions or business needs—that might carry the day.

I'm not saying you have to spend days and days formulating these plans. For each one, you're preparing a talk track that conveys something about your company, how and where your product has succeeded in the past, and how it could be a solution for the customer.

When you're setting out to develop projects to pitch, the best-case scenario is that your Codebreaker, with his inside contacts, already has ideas for likely places your combined efforts will play. If nothing comes right to mind, a little prompting on your part about recent business changes at the customer might spark his mind.

If it seems as if you're going to have to dig a little deeper, start by going to the client's Web site to find out what new product lines are being announced, what companies are being acquired, and what alliances or partnerships are being trumpeted. You can bet that every new aspect of the business will require a back end that will tie seamlessly into the core company, and each one is an opportunity for you.

Lead with the Most Innovative Project

Because every Codebreaker-led meeting with a C-level client is a precious opportunity, it might seem logical to lead with a project proposal that will mean the most revenue for you and your company. But that's not how I always work. Instead, I like to pick the one that is most innovative in its use of a new product or service.

The reason is that, as it's my first time with this new client, I really want to have an interesting conversation with her. If I'm with the Codebreaker, I want to talk about what's important to the Codebreaker as well. If you've done your homework and you understand what's going on today in your market, it's always nice to be able to say, "Have you ever thought about ...?"

I did this with Heinz. We had done Y2K work for them in Australia, so they already knew of us and the fact that we'd done a good job. I called the CIO to set up a meeting, and after hanging up the phone, I realized I wasn't sure what were the best new topics to talk to him about. I phoned back and spoke with his secretary, asking her who their two largest competitors were, and why. I did hours of research on the Web, analyzing first Heinz's Web site, then the competitors.' When I first met with the CIO, I asked him what projects he had on the horizon that could make use of our consulting services again. "Well, Pat, we don't have any new projects coming up soon. But you can call in a year and see what's going on."

So I mentioned to him that I had studied his Web site as well as General Foods,' and I outlined for him some of the key differences I'd found. "Currently you don't have e-procurement facilities on your site, but your two top competitors do. Do you plan on addressing this in the near future?"

He tried to appear unruffled, but I could see he was sitting a little straighter in his chair and leaning a little closer to me. "Yes, actually. We have to look at that soon." The rest of the appointment was taken up with a discussion about the large projects we had done in e-procurement and what his requirements would be.

Sometimes you can bring some interesting conversations to the table to get the client to relax and stop thinking about all the things he has to do, to just chew the fat on something completely different and then come back into other projects. Sometimes the Codebreaker, during her portion of the call, will bring up four or five different avenues you can explore. If you're just there to talk about yourself—I'm going to sell this, I'm going to sell that—you're not going to win. If you're there to seriously and sincerely work on business solutions for this customer, then you want to bring up some interesting possibilities.

If I've heard or read something intriguing in the previous day's *Wall Street Journal*, I might say, "I heard about this project your competitor is doing, and I know it sounds a little far out, but have you ever thought about something similar?" It could turn out to be a nonstarter, of course, but sometimes you'll get an encouraging response and a good conversation. If you plant this kind of seed, you're going to be the owner of that project if it comes to fruition. You have to be very adaptable, but it's always good to go in there with something a little innovative, a little off the mark, because it gets the client talking and leads to a really good, open conversation.

Going into this first sales call, you don't really have to expect to talk more than 5 to 10 minutes about each of your three projects. As we'll see in the next chapter, you're going to let the Codebreaker take the lead in the call, and all you really need are sharp summaries that give the client a chance to get rolling. One of the primary tactical goals in any good sales call is to let the client do 80 percent of the talking. It's almost like leading a witness in court: Talk around the subject area you want to discuss, then start asking specific questions based on the customer's answers.

Be Ready for Inspiration

Although thorough preparation is a must, you have to avoid planning your call to such a degree that you lose all creativity. One time we went to Exide to talk about an e-procurement strategy. The firm had a brand-new CIO who wanted to build an e-procurement system and move on to other things, and I was there to sell him that system.

The meeting started as planned, but when the CIO couldn't explain how other divisions worldwide would be tied into the system, we quickly realized that the company's executives hadn't even been briefed on the need for an overall e-strategy. I ditched my game plan and started probing with open-ended questions: "We will build an e-procurement system for you," we told him, "but how is it going to affect your business? What's your ultimate goal, and how are you going to improve your process to make this feasible? How is it going to improve your company five years from now?" When the CIO realized he couldn't answer those questions, he let us get to work. We went in pitching a $100,000 project that turned into a multimillion-dollar deal. You will close 10 times more revenue if you ask the right kinds of questions.

Preparing for Objections

Objections are a fact of life for every sales rep. But when you're chasing million-dollar deals, the stakes are so high that you can't just try to improvise your way out of them. You've got to be ready with convincing answers to the most common objections before you and your Codebreaker walk into his customer's office.

Below you'll find my suggestions for handling the most frequent, specific objections you'll hear. Take these outlines and write out your own detailed responses, and then practice them just as you did with your 30-second commercial.

"I have no interest in what you're proposing."

If you hear this one, it means you probably haven't addressed any value propositions, either through a lack of research or preparation. It's also possible, though less likely, that you've come up against a customer who likes to test her vendors with tough talk.

The primary task now is to figure out the specific sticking point. You don't want to sputter indignantly and say, "What do you mean by that?" Instead, try: "Are you not interested because you're the wrong person for me to be talking to about it? Or are you not interested because you've found another solution?"

Open-ended questions are crucial. They give you a chance to restate your added value and allow the customer another chance to get it. You're not arguing, but slipping in more facts to get his attention: "I understand you're not interested, but do you think you might be interested in the future, and looking to save 60 percent on your bulk packaging purchases?" Make it positive, leaving the door open for him to reverse himself and say yes. But don't belabor it—if you've made your three best arguments and you're still getting nowhere, this customer just isn't for you, and it's time to bow out gracefully.

If it turns out you're just barking up the wrong tree, you need to salvage the situation by getting the name you should be pursuing: "I'm sorry I was mistaken about your involvement in this project. Would you mind telling me who is handling this for your division so I can talk to him about it?"

"I'm the wrong person."

Sometimes, instead of "I'm not interested," you'll get a startling bit of honesty from a potential client: "I'm the wrong person to talk to about this project." As we saw in the previous example, the obvious response is "Can you tell me who the right person is?"

But sometimes this kind of objection is really just a smokescreen. Customers put up a front on occasion—it's a fact of life. It's usually desperately busy people or ones who are resistant to change who resort to such a tactic; in many cases, you're making more work for these people, especially if they're on salary and already have a large project burden for the next year. In some cases, you might have gotten someone who doesn't really care about business solutions, which means you're at the wrong level.

But if you've done your homework about the company and the project, you should be able to sniff out the truth and salvage the call by asking for another name and offering to take your proposal there.

"I have no money."

Who hasn't heard this one, the most common objection of all? It usually means "I don't understand what the return on investment of your product is for me." Though you don't ever want to bring the hard numbers out first thing, this is the time to present them—but with a subtle lead-in. For example: "You have to understand that I'm not talking right now about a specific contract. What I want to do is to share with you how our warehouse security service actually pays for itself by rapidly cutting down on inventory shrinkage. In fact, our clients typically recoup their initial investment within 90 days." Then match some provable results with a forward-thinking approach: "Not only will you save money quickly, but the ongoing savings will allow you to redirect resources to other inventory management areas."

"We have no projects like that at this time."

If you have an otherwise friendly customer who comes out with this one, I suggest trying this tack: "Does my proposal sound like something you are going to be doing in the next year or two?" It's possible she just wasn't thinking that far ahead, and you now have an opening to talk more. If she says no, however, go for this one: "What projects are currently key to you?" This gives you a chance to propose a solution to a current problem—as long as you know how well your product plays in different areas.

Be aware, though, that you might get a frosty answer: "I'm not going to share that information with you." Companies have been forced to become more and more close-mouthed about their intellectual capital, especially in security matters. Work on a graceful way to pull out of this tense situation if it happens: "I understand. Would you like me to sign a nondisclosure agreement and set up another time to meet?"

"I've never done work with you before." Or "I don't know anything about you or your company."

Avoiding these responses is one of the primary reasons to partner with a Codebreaker—his existing relationship with the client is often enough to keep this objection from coming up. But if it does, agree with the client. It's true, after all. But then turn it around: "However, we've done some great things with Company A and Company B. By the way, do you know John Doe from Company B, where we did a similar project six months ago? If you decide to work with us, I'd be happy to give you his name and number so you can talk about what we did for them."

This can actually be a great objection to get because it opens up the floor for you to present your product's successes. Your differentiator is key here: "You've never done business with us, but you might have done business with other companies that offer similar products. I want to share with you what makes us different."

Another way of handling this objection is to put the client at ease about what you're looking for: "It's true you've never worked with us, and I didn't come in expecting you to give us an expensive, multiyear project. I think we can make a big impact on one of your smaller projects, and then we can talk about more far-ranging work." This is the essence of earning the right to do business with a new customer.

"You don't have enough experience in my vertical market."

Again, you can't deny the facts. But you can quickly redirect the conversation back to your successes: "That's true. However, we've done projects with this product at companies comparable in size to yours." And "size" can mean big or small: Small firms want to know that you won't assume there are layers of management to take care of problems that crop up.

Sometimes you can get creative in this situation. I've had conversations like this: "You know, when Aramark started out, no one had done business with them, either. You might be missing out on an exciting and money-saving idea if you turn away every single new vendor that comes to your door. We have an innovative and successful business solution here. Is it possible that you're being so cautious that you're about to miss out on the next great trend?"

"I've heard some negative things about your product."

This one can be a bit of a heart-stopper, but you have to keep your calm and clarify that it really is your product at issue. The client, who probably blurted this out without thinking, doesn't want you jumping all over this objection, so he may be circumspect about giving you solid information. Start gently: "Can you give me some idea of what you've heard? Sometimes companies are confused." Keep narrowing it down: "What geographic area was it in, and was it in a particular vertical market?" If you're lucky, it will become apparent that the client is in fact confused and you can put him at ease.

If you figure out that he is correct, however, you should try to find out in what specific way: "Was the project handled incorrectly? Were there staff problems?" If you find out it was something besides the product itself, you can say something like "If it has anything to do with personnel problems, we've identified that weakness, and those people are no longer with us. We have brand-new management, and I would challenge anybody to work with these people." (Adapt this for the facts in your particular situation, of course.) If it was indeed the product, it's best to emphasize how it's being improved constantly: "You know, some customers did have issues with version 2.0 of our product, but we are now in version 3.1. Not only have we solved those issues, we've also come out with some enhancements that put us at the forefront of this product segment." It might even help to emphasize how customer feedback—again, if true—has helped to shape later versions of the product.

"We're having so many problems now with layoffs; we don't know where we're going at this time with our company. We might be getting acquired, etc."

It's common to hear this kind of objection nowadays, and you might be right in thinking, "This is a big mess. I'm going to put this on the back burner for a year and come back." But it's important to follow up independently to make sure you aren't being misled by one person's gloomy outlook. Check the business news sites and other contacts you might have at the company or its partners to see if the reality matches the description you've been given. These situations can even be seen as opportunities—you might be looking at a department of 200 people going down to 150, but it's still going to have projects. If you can specify the ROI and efficiency of your project, the right person will see it as pure profit in a downturn.

"I don't see a team here."

This is an objection you and the Codebreaker should anticipate, especially if this is the first time you've partnered. To combat it, highlight the steps you've taken and be forward-looking: "This is the beginning of a strong strategic alliance. Our service technicians are already working together on solutions, and we are marketing together. Let me tell you some of the other ways our products will be working together." Minimize it and move on to something else.

You're now as ready as you'll ever be for the first sales call, so let's get right to it.

Chapter Checklist

To prepare for your first joint sales call with a Codebreaker, you have to:

☐ Schedule an information exchange between your respective tactical teams as soon as you can.

☐ Use the results of that exchange and your other research to brainstorm three likely projects for the target client.

☐ Be ready to lead off with your most interesting project, even if it isn't the one with the highest revenue potential.

☐ Plan the outline of the call, but don't script it to the last detail and lose the spontaneity that can lead to huge deals.

☐ Write out and practice responses to the 10 most common objections you're likely to hear in the call.

The Two Sales Calls

The First Sales Call

Finally, it's time to put theory into practice. All the study, all the research, all the preparation you've undertaken in the previous chapters has readied you for the real proving ground of rapid million-dollar sales—the first sales call.

I've hinted at some of the choreography you and the Codebreaker have to design and practice to run this call effectively, and now I'm going to discuss it in detail, along with the kind of in-the-moment feedback you can anticipate from the client. I'll also clue you into the postcall debriefing session, a priceless learning tool that will help you solidify the results of the current call and sharpen you for the next one.

The Precall Prep

A good Codebreaker will immediately understand the value of preparing for a sales call with you. But it goes beyond simply who's going to say what.

There are really three levels of preparation. The first—figuring out how your products work best together—you've already done when developing the potential projects you're going to present.

The second is determining the best time to reach out to the potential client and securing the meeting. The Codebreaker should, of course, be the one who sets up the sales call with the client—at the moment, this is still her show, and it's her need to see the client on another matter that will most likely get you in the door. But a willing Codebreaker can leverage the advantage of this necessary contact by introducing some of the ideas you intend to discuss with the customer before you even go in there. Many customers like being clued in ahead of time instead of having to take in completely new information on the fly. Giving them a little time to think about their needs can smooth the path of the sales call and result in a more productive first meeting. Not all Codebreakers will be able to arrange this kind of premeeting info session, nor will all customers be interested, but the idea is worth exploring.

As your end of the second prep step, suggest a few possible times to the Codebreaker before she calls to make the appointment. Remember, though, that you're shooting for a big deal here, and if the Codebreaker comes back and says the only slot her customer has open in the next month is Friday at 3:00, be ready to juggle whatever is already on your schedule—there are few other opportunities with as much potential as a Codebreaker-arranged sales call.

When you get the confirmation from the Codebreaker, probe a little bit: "What did the customer say when you asked him about the potential project?" Most times they won't have had a chance to discuss details at all, but once in a while the Codebreaker will really have connected and it might be that the customer will be bringing three other people to the meeting. (I've actually had up to eight or nine people at a first meeting—now *those* are interested customers.) It's important to get the names and telephone numbers of everyone attending ahead of time so that you can briefly introduce yourself by phone and offer to answer any questions that crop up in the week before the meeting. You'll have made a human connection that will make the meeting flow more easily—they'll actually greet you as if they know you, because you reached out to make them feel comfortable. Finding out the roles of the others who are coming to the meeting might prompt you to bring along a member of your tactical team as well.

The third kind of preparation takes place just before you actually go into the meeting together. You need to nail down the roles— what is each one of you going to do in the call? The Codebreaker is going to take the lead, but you can't let her dominate the agenda. A successful, big-ego Codebreaker, if she really gets rolling, can just forget you're there.

This almost happened to me when I was working with a Codebreaker from a top software firm. During a dress rehearsal for our first-ever call together, I discovered that he couldn't stop singing his company's praises long enough to frame for the customer how our products would be working together. These timing issues have to be hashed out and agreed to mutually, so I suggested an equal-time split: "You've got the first 20 minutes so you can talk about your two items of interest, and then I'm going to talk for the next 20."

Make it clear that you don't want the Codebreaker jumping in during your presentation. I've had to train some Codebreakers not to answer questions on the client's behalf! I appreciate the kind of close relationship that makes such a thing possible, but it really just slows things down and takes the focus away from my product. You, of course, should pay the Codebreaker the same courtesy during her presentation.

The day of the call, I usually like to meet to go over all the ground rules again to make sure they're fresh in both our minds— people forget what they talked about yesterday, let alone three weeks ago. I learned this the hard way. One time, a Codebreaker and I hadn't spoken for about 10 days before a client meeting. After the customer spent about 5 minutes explaining his business requirement, the Codebreaker used up our remaining 40 minutes talking about an irrelevant solution, and I couldn't get him to stop. If we'd been able to get together ahead of time, I would have refreshed his memory about the plan we'd agreed to and perhaps kept the call from going bad.

Meet at a quiet place near the customer's office an hour before-hand to sit down and chat a little—it helps both of you to loosen up so that you'll appear natural together. If you're bringing a technical or service person along to the call, it allows the Codebreaker to meet and get comfortable with him, too. This premeeting briefing also ensures that your Codebreaker isn't going to show up late—whether for some mundane reason like a traffic tie-up or flat tire or because you're dealing with a high-powered personality who thinks arriving in the customer's office with five minutes to spare is early.

Once you're clear about what the agenda is for the call and who is going to take on what role, you can just get up and head right to the client's office together.

The Codebreaker Takes the Lead

A Codebreaker is never going to take you to see one of his clients for the heck of it—he's already got either something to discuss about an existing project or some new information he believes the client needs to know now. So, after you're introduced, you're going to step into the background and let the Codebreaker use his allot-ted time as he needs.

As was agreed, you're not interjecting yourself into the conver-sation. Instead, you're on the edge of your seat, taking in every-thing. Usually, there's some pretty good information being shared about current projects and even the general working style at the client's company. Listen for a few salient points that, when it's your turn, you can refer back to and use as ways to lead the conversa-tion where you want it to go. Unearthing one or two of those points is like hitting a home run.

When I was new at sales, I used to take notes in these face-to-face situations—if you're still a relative rookie yourself, you might have to. But I learned to let the information burn into my mind because I discovered how important it is to keep an eye on the customer and observe how he relates to the Codebreaker. Scan the office now and again to see what you can deduce about the client. Does he have brainteaser puzzles on his desk or a spreadsheet on his computer monitor? You're probably looking at an analytical personality, someone who will be sure to take an extra-hard look at your numbers. Are there more awards for team achievements than individual ones? This client is most likely quite personable and eager to find a solution that works for everyone. What kind of sports trophies do you see? How about the photos—more family or business? I'm not suggesting that you gawk for minutes at a time, of course, but some subtle glances while the Codebreaker is making his pitch can yield advantageous information.

Mistakes Codebreakers Make

- Monopolizing the customer.
- Not allowing you to talk about what you need to talk about.
- Being ignorant of your product or the way each product complements the other.
- Being unclear about the importance of your product to the customer at this time.

The Handoff and Your Opening

Once the Codebreaker has finished with the heart of his presentation, he has to bring you into the conversation. The customer is sitting there in a state of pleasant expectation, having wondered ever since you first shook hands what you were going to bring to the table. A really good Codebreaker will heighten this expectation by reiterating your recent accomplishments: "He has done some incredible things at Company X and Company Y, and that's why I thought it was important for you to meet him." That might sound a bit forced, but don't forget, the Codebreaker's goal here is to prove additional worth to the customer. He's already delivered something new about his product, and now he should make it clear that he believes bringing you here is just as important.

Once you get the handoff, I suggest starting off by recounting one of the Codebreaker's recent accomplishments, using it to show why you thought a partnership between your companies was a winning proposition for customers. Depending on how well the Codebreaker gave an indication of the breadth of your company's experience, you might have to improvise and add some compelling details before launching into the main part of your opening—a longer, more solution-based version of your 30-second commercial.

Providing a simple verbal description of the product is paramount. The customer might have looked at your Web site for five minutes when he first heard about you three weeks ago, but he's long since forgotten. (It's very rare that I get a customer who's as prepared for that meeting as we are—but that's why sales professionals exist, right?) For example, when I was selling knowledge management software, I explained it as a product that automatically collected the millions of bits of information that flowed into a company every day and organized it by department, division, project, or client, all the while saving hundreds of man-hours per day. With that quick nontechnical explanation, knowledge management suddenly made sense to potential clients. It took a lot of practice to reach that point, but it's absolutely necessary. Depending on the kind of product you're selling, it's great to wrap up with "And that's just one of the primary strengths of the software. It can also do …" A mention of one or two other applications can get the customer thinking about how the product might match his requirements.

The length of the opening is crucial. Talking straight through to a C-level client for more than five or six minutes will mark you as a second-rater who lectures to clients instead of listening. You want to provide enough information to give the client a positive initial impression of your worth and encourage him to open up to you about his pressing needs and wants.

The Dialogue

If your opening has been compelling, the customer should start throwing questions at you when you pause to take a breath: "Where has this product been used in the past?" or "What are some of its other applications?"

You need to listen now; you're trying to get him to talk more, so you ask leading questions about current needs, future needs, how certain things work. If the name of one of your competitors comes up in the discussion, don't ask whether the product worked well— focus on the requirement the customer was trying to solve with the competitor's product, because refined and new requirements are where your opportunity lies. All this shared information will form the basis of the project for which you will seek a green light at the end of your 20 minutes.

If your presentation hasn't kicked off the conversation for some reason, though, it's time to reach into your bag of spares and talk about another of your product's applications. You're not trying to run this as *Let's Make a Deal*—"Stop me if you hear something you like"—but you can bring up a third possibility if the second one doesn't cause the dialogue to catch fire.

But if the third one falls flat, you'll have no choice but to come out and ask pointedly leading questions. Continuing to use knowledge management software as an example, these might be: What is your focus for knowledge management for this company? Where do you think it has the most play? How do you handle that task now? In reality, sometimes C-level clients don't know that much about the details of particular business segments, and I wouldn't expect them to—they're running huge companies. Break it down into the simplest terms that they can understand from their business solutions standpoint: "Here's what we've done in the past for other clients; here's what the product is capable of doing; and for our last three customers we were able to price it so that it paid for itself 90 days after it was installed. After that, it's been incredibly profitable because it gives them leading-edge information faster than their competitors. Do you have any place where it would be of benefit to you?"

If you've gotten to this point without some significant feedback, you've got nothing to lose by just asking flat out: "What are your top three projects for the next year?" If that doesn't start a dialogue, nothing will.

All these suggestions are meant, of course, as gambits to move the conversation along; if you've done your homework properly, what you hear back shouldn't surprise you. Once in a while, though, people will stun you. Once, in a Codebreaker meeting, I asked a vice president of a large telecommunications company what his top three concerns were. Number one wasn't increasing revenue in a certain business segment, as I had expected, but keeping his current client base. I was shocked, but I recovered quickly enough to make a case for how my software would help him learn more about his customers and what made them tick. Even if I had looked at the Web for six weeks, I never would have found out his number-one goal without asking the question.

Surprises That Can Crop Up

Before we get to the wrap-up, I'm going to take a few moments to review the best ways to handle some of the surprises that can suddenly confront you as you're ushered into the client's office.

Sometimes you might arrive at the appointment to find an attendee you weren't expecting, perhaps a technical or service person who's defensive about the fact that you're even there. The best approach in this situation is just to maintain your cool, stick to the game plan as much as possible, and make it clear that you are there to benefit their entire company; this calm approach will weaken the effect of any negative attitudes he's displaying in front of his boss. Try to keep the conversation between you and the executive as much as you can, while still answering any legitimate questions the interloper might have.

On the other hand, you could have a mystery attendee who's really interested in your product. One of the times this happened to me, I ended up extending the meeting to four hours as various people with different needs came in and out of the meeting at the CEO or CIO's request. By the end of the meeting, we had built the statement of work for the project.

Customers will often test you. A good C-level executive has a lot riding on his reputation and his company's success. Especially if you're from a smaller company, it only makes sense that he's got to be sure you're capable of handling his requirements and that your people are of a high enough caliber to work with his. But it's usually done in a positive way: "I need to know more about you and your company before I can commit."

Other times, you can just see that the client has had a bad experience somewhere along the way. If you pick up on this vibe, the best way to defuse it is to confront it: "I get the impression that you've been burned in the past. Tell me about that." Usually, this is enough to get him to open up a little and share his concerns, which are often related to deadlines and money, and which you can alleviate by assuring him of your company's shared-risk policy or whatever is appropriate to the specific situation. (I believe more sales professionals should include shared-risk policies in their contracts—it's an insurance policy for success for any client and helps close deals much faster.)

And sometimes you get grilled because of the client's personality. Some decision makers need to mix it up a little when doing business. There's not a lot you can do in this case, but roll with it until he knows you better. Whatever the motivation behind the grilling, your goal should be to convince the customer that he should regard you as a problem solver, not a vendor. You're not there to sell him something he doesn't need, but to provide a high-quality solution that's going to benefit his company.

The End of the Call and Action Items

The fundamental goal of this first meeting is to prove your worth to a potential client, so that even if you walk out of that room with no hope of a project right now, this customer knows it's in her interest to keep in touch with you and open her door freely the next time you approach her with an idea. To improve your chances for further communication, neutralize whatever negatives might crop up using the techniques we discussed in the last chapter.

Ideally, at the end of 20 minutes you and the customer have jointly identified a pressing business need for which you can provide a solution. Is he going to sign a deal right then and there? That would be great, but it doesn't often happen—products are so specialized now that decision makers need input from people with the right expertise before they can give the go-ahead. Instead, you're going to try to get two things: the name of the person who is heading up the project you want to work on, and a firm date for your next meeting with the C-level exec—the one where you're going to finalize the deal.

As you can imagine, the most straightforward way to find out the project head is just to ask: "Who's heading up this project? I'd like to get as much information as I can to tailor our solution." It turns out Lynn Hayes is going to be your contact. What you want to find out next is whether the project has an official name, so that you can use it in your communications. And finally, put them together in the big request: "Would you mind letting Lynn know that you've asked me to contact her about Project X? And could you please copy me in on the e-mail? Then I will follow up with her on Monday." (And call whether he e-mails or not, to keep the momentum going!)

It's a little trickier to arrange a firm date for your next meeting because at this point you really don't know how much back-and-forth it's going to take between your staff and the client's to customize your presentation. Plus, it's a meeting that must be attended by both staffs and the exec himself. I like to shoot for about two weeks in these situations, which gives my people enough breathing room to do a sterling job on their research but isn't so long that the client starts to think about other things.

Once you have a date, end the meeting with a forward-looking statement: "I'm going to meet with Lynn and learn more about your project to see if it's a good fit." Don't assume that you've identified a perfect match yet. Customers like it when you leave things open-ended—it reinforces for them that your primary mission is not to sell widgets, but to provide solutions.

The Debriefing

Once the meeting is over and you've said your goodbyes to the client, you're not quite done yet. It's time to find a quiet corner, sit down with the Codebreaker, and take half an hour to go over the call. Codebreakers can sometime be reluctant to do this—they want to move on to their next appointment—but it's essential that you build in this time. It's not a gab session, but a directed discussion with a standard series of questions that will actually benefit both of you:

- "This is what I think I heard; what did you hear?" You want the Codebreaker to relate his impressions because you might get a different take on the call.

- "Tell me what the customer meant by this. I wasn't clear on what he was talking about." The topic might not have had anything to do with you, but it's a way to learn more about the Codebreaker's dealings with this customer.

- "What do you think the customer thought about the product? What do you think I could have done better?" I always want to know how I could have been better on a sales call.

- "How do you think we did together? How do you think the meeting went from a tactical viewpoint versus a strategic? Did we accomplish our goals?"

- "Is there anything we need the client to clarify?" If you and the Codebreaker both feel there's something that's been left unsaid, you want to find out right away—the worst thing you can do is start down the wrong path. If you're contemplating a true joint project, suggest that the Codebreaker e-mail the client and copy you in. If it's not a dual job, you'll have to get the information yourself.

If the call went extremely well and there's already a skeleton proposal on the table, the debriefing could turn into a planning session and go longer. Most of the time, though, it's just an opportunity to clear up any confusion that might have arisen, decide action items for the next step with the client, and hone the approach for the next call you make together.

From here, it's time to go back to the office and get together with your tactical team to make sure the great ideas you've just created can be turned into reality and revenue!

Chapter Checklist

To have a successful first sales call, you have to:

☐ Fulfill the three levels of preparation: Figure out how your product fits best with the Codebreaker's, pick the optimal time for and secure the client meeting, and sit down and review the ground rules with the Codebreaker before the sales call.

☐ Lay out a mutually agreeable agenda with the Codebreaker, aiming for an equal time split, and schedule a precall run-through to make sure she's not going to get carried away with her own eloquence and forget you're there.

☐ Let the Codebreaker take the lead, and use that time to glean useful information about his client.

☐ Keep your opening to five minutes or less so that the client has plenty of time to ask you questions and share his business needs.

☐ Ask for specific project information at the end of the call, and promise to follow up quickly.

☐ Make the Codebreaker sit down immediately after the call and debrief with you—you both have to be on the same page to make the rest of the process run smoothly.

The Reality Check and Preparing for the Second Sales Call

By now there's a plum project nearly in your grasp, and it's a natural impulse to want to push ahead with all possible speed to get the deal closed. But what you really need to do is take a quick breather and make sure your competencies match the requirements that were revealed in the first sales call. To start this chapter, we're going to pull back a little to examine the importance of connecting with the client's project manager to set up an information exchange between its team and yours, which will help your side make sure you can provide the promised solution, even if it involves bringing in other partners to cover areas of weakness.

Assuming that this reality check results in a green light internally, you'll have to determine who will be part of the proposal team on a day-to-day basis and set a breakdown of responsibilities. (If this is a joint project, you'll also need to involve the Codebreaker's team in this preparation.) You and your team members will also be engaging in some sleuthing to figure out exactly which of the client's decision makers and influencers need to be in on the conference call loop as you prepare your strategy. Rounding out the approach are tips on keeping your sales manager and other reps from bombarding your new contacts before the first deal is even closed.

Staying focused on requirements is of course a primary goal, but we'll also begin to explore the idea of how pricing strategies can help reps who are selling tangible goods move additional units while staying true to that principle.

What Kind of Stakeholder Are You?

As we pass the halfway mark to a million-dollar deal, we have to answer one crucial question: Who owns the project? There are two possible positive outcomes when you pitch with a Codebreaker—you're going to come out either a majority stakeholder or a minority stakeholder. If you're the majority, you've either made an agreement to provide the solution by yourself or with the Codebreaker's firm playing a supporting role. If you're the minority, the roles are reversed, and your team will take a back seat to the Codebreaker's team.

The first time out with a new Codebreaker, you'll often find yourself in the second category. It's an admirable position to be in, one that gives you an excellent opportunity to prove your worth to the client and earn the right to do big business on your own down the road. For the purposes of the rest of the book, however, we're going to assume that you're the majority stakeholder in the project.

Making Connections

As I discussed briefly in the previous chapter, your immediate goal is to arrange a meeting with the manager of the project you're trying to win—we're calling her Lynn Hayes. You've been treated to the corporate view of the project's strategic importance, and now it's time to gather information on Lynn's more hands-on level.

You asked the executive you met with to copy you in on any communication he's sent to Lynn, so when you get your copy of the e-mail, send a message to her right away listing the dates and times you're available; you're aiming for a meeting with her as soon as possible—certainly within a week. Be sure to copy the boss right back in, so that Lynn sees that everything she does with you is going to him. (As a general rule, this is an excellent way to stay on a C-level client's scope—every time he e-mails you, send something back: "Thank you for the update; I'm following up.")

What kind of information should you ask for when you get to talk? In addition to any pertinent technical details, try to uncover some of the wider issues of the project—the names of all the departments that will be affected, the revenue to the client if it succeeds or fails, and anything else that could influence your solution.

Sometimes you might sense some resistance from a project manager during your first contact, especially if the manager has been dealing with another vendor on similar kinds of projects. I try to make it clear right up front that I'm not there to dethrone any vendor who's already doing great work, and that I'm there to make those people better with a product or service that supports theirs. Dispelling the assumption that you're just coming in to sweep out all the work that's already been done will go a long way in creating trust. Of course, you might find that the project manager (PM) can't stand the vendors she's been working with, which leaves you a wide-open opportunity to fix a long-standing problem. This happened to me at a major telecommunications firm—I made another million-dollar sales deal just because the PM didn't like the other rep!

The Preproposal

Once you've established an initial rapport with the project manager, you will be creating a preproposal—a one- or two-page document that states the requirements as you understand them from your initial sales call and lays out a simplified version of your proposed solution. I know this sounds like one of those things you read in a book and nobody actually does—but it's crucial, both internally and for the customer.

In your synopsis you'll start the ball rolling with just a couple of paragraphs recounting the sales call: I met with X, here's what she needs, here's what I think we can do for her. Next, send this around to your tactical team members to bring them into the loop on the potential project and let them add their thoughts and suggestions. When you are working with people who work well with others, they pool their intelligence and come up with something 10 times better than any one of the members could have come up with on his own.

Take the best from each person's work and finalize the document. Don't let them turn it into some abstract masterwork at this point—all that's required is a brief restatement of the problem and an overview of your solution. The goal for completion of this preproposal is two days—a lack of speed can kill the deal. It doesn't always happen this rapidly, especially the first couple of times it's needed, but as your team grows together, you'll find it easier to assemble it quickly.

After all of your tactical team members have had their say, you'll use this preproposal to discover the names of all the client's people who will either be working on the project or involved in evaluating it. Because client decision makers who have probably never heard of your company or your product will be seeing this, you need to include some background information but not hard numbers or deadlines.

Once you've sent this document to the project manager, you're looking for two kinds of feedback: first, suggestions or clarifications regarding the project requirements from the manager; second, and most important, the names and contact information of everyone the PM forwarded the document to. This is your opening into the level at which the real details of the project will be handled—seize this opportunity early in the process to introduce yourself to each person. The best way is simply to call and ask whether they received the information and if they have any questions. You can e-mail the information, but a personal call is required here. Often you're going to get voice mail, but even if you do get through to the real person, it's almost a certainty that there won't be any questions yet because he or she probably won't have read the document. Your call serves as a friendly reminder to bump that task up the to-do list, makes you a known entity, and smoothes the way for calls your team will place.

Once the preproposal gets around to all the concerned parties, you'll want to schedule a conference call between them and your staff. It's preferable to gather everyone together in the flesh, but I've learned that working with so many different schedules inevitably slows down the process and blows the time frame. It can take six weeks to coordinate a face-to-face meeting, but a conference call can be put together in a week or less, especially if you slate it for 8:00 a.m. to 9:00 a.m., when everyone is fresh and not likely to be in another meeting. Your role during this call will be to direct the conversation to the areas most relevant to the heart of the project; in other words, let your staff talk, but keep them focused.

After this conference call, you and your team will know whether you can deliver the winning solution and whether you'll need to bring in any outside help on certain requirements. I have always deferred to my technical people on these kinds of decisions, but if it becomes necessary to seek out other vendors to supplement your own offering, try to look through your list of potential Codebreakers first—imagine how good an impression you'll make if your first contact is to discuss a bid on an active project! If, however, it turns out you really can't handle the job, there's no shame in being upfront with the client. Who is likely to gain more respect, a vendor that bows out gracefully before money is committed or a company that gets in over its head and wastes millions of client dollars on a faulty product?

But we're going to assume here that the process has worked as intended and everyone is agreed on how to proceed. Inevitably, there will be more conference calls as you and your team refine the full-scale presentation that you'll present at the second sales call.

We'll talk more about what comprises that presentation and who should attend in the next chapter. I don't know if it's become apparent yet, but the sales rep has really reached a crossroads by this point in the process. Your job is starting to shift away from discovery and persuasion to administration and coaching. Keeping the lines of communication clear and the team's momentum going is up to you—you're the one with the timeline in your head. Of course, the longer you've worked with your team, the less micromanagement you'll be obligated to provide, but don't be surprised if you have to have a bit of a heavy hand in the beginning—no one will have the same sense of urgency as you. And don't count on anyone else sharing your strategic vision of where this first big deal can take you—especially your company's whole sales force.

Holding Back Your Colleagues

By this point in the book, you know the importance of being a client-oriented solution provider when you're trying to make million-dollar sales. These opportunities don't come along every day, and they take careful management to bring off successfully. But it's also true that once it becomes apparent to your sales manager and colleagues that you've got an inside line on such a big deal, they all start piling on.

It doesn't take long for everyone from the executive vice president on down to swamp you with e-mails asking what's going on and when you're going to close. Or for higher-ups to whisper, "Make sure you give this guy a role in the project" and "We're underperforming on supply chain—stick some in there." Or for a rep who works with your potential client in another region to insist he fly in and sit in on your meetings. Sometimes even the technical folks try to horn in.

One time I had a gentleman, the boss of two tactical team members, who was so jealous that he would try to go in to see the customers without us. He thought he could sell and insisted on being copied in on all the e-mails, and even started phoning the customers and setting up appointments to go out there and talk to them about the project. He almost ended up ruining a deal with his meddling.

I called the customer to follow up, and he asked me: "Why are all these people from your company calling me up? I thought I was dealing with you." It made us look unprofessional and as though we had no internal communication. Why would he trust us with one of his valuable projects when we can't even manage our own people? I flew in and closed the first phase of the deal for $300,000 before it imploded and got the technical manager taken off the account.

This kind of situation can be even worse if you're at a company that gives technical people quotas because they want it to look as though they closed the deal. Technical and service people are not sales professionals, nor are sales reps techs. I've run into many companies that think they are interchangeable. What's the end result? A slowed-down sales cycle, client confusion, and fewer closes. You need both kinds of team members, acting within their clearly defined roles, to close million-dollar deals successfully.

The problem of piling on arises in large part because many salespeople have to fill out weekly prospect forms. Though reps complain about the forms all the time, I'm not totally against them—after all, they do fulfill a valuable function in helping you coordinate with your team; if they're all in working in Wyoming for two weeks, you know not to schedule an intensive work period—but there's no denying the fact that they broadcast your activities.

So what can you do about this possibly deal-killing interference? There's always a certain amount that you just have to live with—that's office politics. But to minimize it, start your internal selling early. As soon as you know you're moving into a preproposal phase, get the word out to everyone at the office: "I am working on a potentially big deal, and I need some space and time to secure it." Ask around to detect looming conflicts over the availability of your people, and find out how you can support them when they're switching over from another rep's project to yours.

When other reps are climbing on, the most effective thing to do is take it right to the sales manager and demand that it stop: "It's not the right time to bring someone else in. Let me close this deal first, and then I will take in people who are selling other products. Doing this before the close of my deal will confuse the customer and possibly blow any chance we have." The better your track record, the more likely your word will carry weight.

With executives, it's not that simple. Unless you're buddies with the president of the company, there's no higher authority you can appeal to, so you have to make that argument yourself in a more politic way: "I want to be realistic about our chances if we pursue the swarming strategy you're suggesting. Taking five people into my next meeting is not going to contribute to the trust I've begun to build with this customer. He doesn't need a $200,000 CRM module right now, and trying to slip it in could cost us the whole deal. I have a plan that is halfway to scoring us a large new customer. Once we've proven ourselves, we can spread the opportunities around."

My old approach was to keep as much information as possible to myself, but I started getting dinged for that by top management. Business has changed so much in the past 10 years that you're never going to be left completely alone. Executive offices are crawling with experts and consultants, and you just have to smile, thank them for the input, and explain later why you didn't follow it. By that point you'll have gotten the deal and can use your success as a defense.

As more of your selling time is devoted to million-dollar deals, you're going to have to help foster an environment where sales, tech, and execs work together from the get-go. Top corporate management should encourage such cooperation, but they don't always. Often they've never been in sales or just don't understand tech people, so they don't recognize that setting the two groups against one another with quotas can actually work against revenue goals.

The more successfully you follow the Codebreakers program, the higher the pressure will undoubtedly be, but you have to hold the line with everything you have, for the sake of your company and your clients.

Pricing Homework

Throughout the book, and in this chapter especially, we have examined the importance of keeping customer requirements in the forefront of our planning. But as others on your team start to adopt that responsibility, you as the sales rep have to concentrate on coming up with the numbers that will make this deal work while maximizing the company's—and your own—earnings.

In consulting work, upselling opportunities abound; we'll talk about them in greater detail in the next chapter. For the time being, I'd like to address reps who handle tangible goods, because they will have to demonstrate the bottom line more quickly.

The amount of internal work you'll have to do when developing these kinds of projects will depend on whether you're doing a small one-off deal or something over a few hundred thousand dollars. If you're just doing a one-off, internal people aren't going to have too much to do with you. But if you're big enough to get their attention, you can count on needing to convince them that a price break will help the deal.

With some companies, there's a price list without much variance, so you don't ever want to go in with your best deal. Instead, lead off with the list price and negotiate from there, leaving a minimum of 15 percent play factor to make it a win-win situation. Customers today are taught effective negotiating techniques to handle vendors, so they are always asking, "What else can you do for me?" or telling you you're in a competitive situation even if you're not to try to get you down 10 or 15 percent. Hey, it's smart business—just make sure you're smarter.

If you have enough information to know the customer's required price point but your normal discount off the list isn't anywhere close, you have to take the fight inside your own company. If you think you have a serious customer, start the pricing ball rolling early—a big deal can disappear during the weeks spent trying to get permission for a nonstandard discount from a distant corporate headquarters.

I was faced with a similar situation at one of my former employers. In putting together a $1.2 million knowledge management software consulting project for an international legal firm, I found that I needed to get a pricing exception to cement the deal. We already had a software maintenance contract for that firm, and one of our VPs said, "Let's fold the old maintenance contract into the new one to leverage the discount." I didn't want him to do that—I didn't need the leverage to close the new deal—but he insisted on complicating matters. I had to go to corporate in England to get permission. By the time the head office got back to us, our company had laid off 20 percent of our software developers and the legal firm's parent company got word. They came back to us and said, "How can we trust you with this deal if we don't even know that you're going to be able to produce new versions of the software and maintain what we already have?" I think you can imagine what the outcome was.

You don't want to walk in quoting list prices on one million dollars worth of products or services, but you do still want some leverage. This way, when talk finally turns to cost, you can tell the customer, "I want to earn the right to do business with you; I'm going to price this to win, not just throw out a bunch of figures at you."

If you don't have any idea of the magic price point, you will have to dig a little harder on the client side. Some of them play it pretty close to the vest, holding out to see how well the product performs on a small scale. But in that situation, a good rep will ask leading questions about other divisions or locations that might be able to use the same equipment: "I will work with you to get the best price possible to take care of your immediate needs, but let me ask whether you might have another facility or location that would benefit from having our products (or services) in place. If I could get you a great break on 125 units instead of 100, would you be able to put them to good use?" And if you elicit a positive response, you're going to turn around and present the case to your pricing people that's there's value in placing more units with the customer and crowding out the competition.

More on pricing psychology later. Now let's begin our look at the second sales call with the elements of a dynamic presentation.

Chapter Checklist

To do a realistic competency assessment for a potential project and get ready for the second sales call, you have to:

☐ Decide whether you're a majority or a minority stakeholder in the project.

☐ Write up a one- to two-page preproposal to circulate among your tactical team.

☐ Submit the polished preproposal to the client's project manager and find out who it's been copied to on the client's side—these are the influencers and decision makers you need to win over.

☐ Keep sales colleagues and executives from horning in on your breakthrough—the deal depends on it.

☐ Assess your pricing strategy and make internal inquiries if you think you might need a nonstandard discount.

The Second Sales Call

You've now reached the final major hurdle on the path to a million-dollar deal: the second sales call. By this point in the process, especially in consulting or other service situations, you have taken a backseat to the technical staff, but your role is far from over. In addition to keeping the project's overall momentum going, you will need to run the large-scale presentation that's the focus of this chapter. If you can pull it off in such a way that the client's team members are nodding their heads every time you address a requirement, by the time you walk out of that conference room, the rest of the process will seem like a minor detail.

Setting Up the Call

The first issue to address is the timing of the second sales call. Projects that the client sees as critical—even if they aren't slated to begin until the next quarter or the new year—necessitate rapid responses. Companies try to stay on top of innumerable details and like to anticipate all the problems up front; help them out by aiming for a second sales call two weeks after the first call. When they reach out early for expert advice, they don't always get the responses they expect or are hoping for, and the earlier you can enter a process, the more chance you have to control its direction. Hit while your information is fresh in the client's mind.

When you contact the director or project manager to set up this call, find out the names of everyone who is being invited—there might be four or five, or even more, on the client's side of the table at this meeting. It's especially important to identify the influencers—usually the hard-core tech representatives who are actually going to build the solution side by side with your people. (Your team members can help you with this—more than likely, they'll have some idea of whom to contact from their introductory work on the preproposal.) Tapping into the influencers' knowledge base both before and during the call will improve your solution greatly—they will know in an instant whether your plans will work or clash with the client's existing systems.

Another important invitee is the C-level executive you met with originally. His schedule might be less accommodating than those of your other attendees, and you might have to give up on the idea if waiting for him would require postponing the meeting for more than a couple of weeks. Still, the advantages are great—there's hardly a better way to strengthen the good feeling you produced in the first meeting than to present a well-conceived solution just a few weeks later.

Once you've figured out the lineup for the other side, huddle with your tactical team to pick the right people to sit on your side. (Remember the last chapter's warnings against letting others pile on—everyone you bring with you should have something valuable to contribute to the project at hand.) When you've accomplished this, send all the members a written overview of the project and who's going to be in the meeting. Sketch out a plan for who will present which elements of your solution, and then let everyone weigh in.

As the basis of the presentation, of course, you'll use the preproposal you created in the last chapter. Your team members will already have fleshed it out with a number of details from their information exchange with the client's personnel. In fact, it was routine for my team members to have daily conference calls with the customer as the time for the second call approached—we wanted to make sure that we had thought through every possible question and objection we might face.

To ensure the appropriateness of your solution, it's key to try to get the client's internal documentation about the project. The most professional companies produce 5- to 10-page business plans—with phases, descriptions of existing modules, timelines, and specific concerns—that are detailed enough to justify a multimillion-dollar budget. If you can get your hands on this, you're in great shape—it will dictate the form of the statement of work you hope to contract for at the end of the call. But do proceed with some caution. One project I put together for a large financial concern was incredibly complicated. We were sent a document that turned out to be the upfront work for a request for pricing. It gave us a lot of detail, but much of it had been created months previously, and we couldn't assume that everything was still valid as we set about matching the requirements.

Along the same lines, it's important to determine which aspects of a project are the most important, and see which of these crucial components best match up with your core competencies. Many times you can't do everything in a project, and you have to determine whether you're going to position yourself as the solution provider who will bring in partners to cover in those areas, or just as a vendor who will handle important parts of a project under someone else's direction.

Of course, it's almost a certainty that before you're allowed to see any internal documents about the project you're trying to close, you will be asked to sign a nondisclosure agreement (NDA). No director is going to discuss just any project with you because a lot of sales reps are big blabbermouths who might call up two of their partners and say, "Can you guess what XYZ Company is getting ready to do?" Who can take that chance?

Once you've executed the NDA, copy in everyone you've contacted about the project so that all are informed of your status. You might even want to be the one who suggests that an NDA be drawn up and signed—it's an excellent way, as a vendor, to show you're responsible.

Preparing the Presentation

Every conversation you have with a project manager, every specific question you have asked and the resulting response, should be put into writing and e-mailed to your team. Whether it's 2:00 in the afternoon or 10:00 at night, type it up and send it out while it's fresh in your mind (and, of course, keep a copy for your own reference). Everyone's ideas, thoughts, and questions should be shared in the same way. This enables a lot of levels of consultation to happen simultaneously—you and the project manager, you and your team, your team and their team, and so on. All this information needs to be evaluated for inclusion in the project summary for the presentation, because making a point of including specific requirement information that didn't come up during the initial sales call but that you acquired later from technical discussions shows a great understanding of your value-add role. You're actually telling the exec about this project in a more concise and solution-oriented way than her own people are able to.

At the same time, you're continuing to focus on the value-add part of your role—the more innovative, the better. You and your team are building a solution that will maximize benefit to the customer, something that is going to be a solution not just for today, but that anticipates and solves something they hadn't even thought of. You'll be amazed at the impact this has.

Your team leaders will distill this information into a compelling PowerPoint presentation. The aim of this walk-through should not be to unveil the perfect solution, but to spur a wide-ranging discussion between you and the client that will make it perfect in time for the close. The worst thing to do in the presentation is to try to present a finished solution that can't be changed, because even with the client's internal documentation and a couple of good technical conference calls, you might not have all the information yet.

A lot of reps lose the deal in a second sales call by saying: "We've got it solved. Here's what we're going to do for you." Instead, your approach should be more open-ended: "Based on the information you've already given us, we're leaning toward this solution. What do you think about this idea?" It's an invitation to information sharing on both sides. The best presentation meetings I've been a part of were those in which the client's project manager welcomed my technical person's expertise; good project managers are always looking for help.

Preparing the team for the presentation is much like preparing with the Codebreaker before the first sales call. With team input, you've already assigned certain segments of the presentation to the appropriate person; now, instruct team members (and alliance partners, if any) not to interrupt one another. This means that you shouldn't interject, either—you are done selling, and whether this deal flies is now largely out of your hands.

Let me stress here the importance of running a full dress rehearsal if you have doubts about any of the participants. One time, at Johnson & Johnson, we needed a third-party provider to complete our solution, and we wanted to project seamless integration to the customer. We started the rehearsal with various people in our organization running through their PowerPoint presentations. When it was Jim's turn to deliver his company's portion, he started grandstanding. He was trying to seize his opportunity in front of high-level corporate people to establish his own product—but if he'd done that for real, he would have lost the chance to get in there as part of our successful project. We explained to him the benefits and value of showing a unified business solution to the customer. He understood and toned it down, and we won the business. If we had not made time for a rehearsal, we would all have been sunk.

I always personally reviewed the entire PowerPoint presentation before the second sales call. There were times when my team did a great technical job but didn't answer all the implied questions in the client's requirements. Usually it's because the service team felt they couldn't address certain aspects—but you can't just say that to a client. If you can't perform certain pieces of the solution, you'd better partner with somebody who can, even if it means delaying the presentation.

Selling Up

Before we get to the call, I'd like to take a minute to examine a selling opportunity that is sometimes missed. If, in analyzing the customer's requirements for the presentation, you discover that the proposed budget can't support the entire solution, one of the best ways to avoid losing that business to another vendor is to propose building it in phases.

Let's say that your team has determined that implementing the customer's full wish list on a particular project will cost $3 million, but the budget is only $1 million. Your first phase, then, should handle the essentials of the project for that price (if this is technically feasible, of course). But along with that, you will also introduce the idea of phases two and three, in which all of the remaining requirements plus a few extras for good measure can be implemented for an additional $1 million each. As long as you can submit honest, compelling explanations to the client about the need to split the project into phases, you stand an excellent chance of bringing in the larger amount. While you work on delivering the main part of what the project requires, thereby making everyone look good, the manager can work to influence his budgeting process to make room for additional phases that will make the baseline solution even more productive to his company.

Even if you can construct the full solution for the budgeted price, you should consider adding another phase to talk about during the sales call that brings additional functionality to the project. It offers the possibility of more revenue and keeps your billable personnel in the account longer, which is good for your company, and allows you to demonstrate higher value-add by fine-tuning and improving your solution, which is good for your reputation.

In the Call

After everyone's settled in and ready to begin, you'll kick off the proceedings. The first quarter of the presentation is just a brief overview of your company; you might have already sent the attendees to your Web site, but if they looked at it at all, it was for 10 minutes at 7:30 the morning of the presentation. Help them out with a few minutes on your strengths and past successes—a review of your company's other core competencies could lead to future projects.

"We're here today to discuss the way Brightstation's knowledge management software can be used by Derwent to categorize patents. Our goal is to review the accuracy, speed, and efficiency of categorizing patents electronically versus doing the same thing manually.

"Our first few minutes will highlight projects we've done in the past and what the results were. For example, at Thomson Scientific, they used our software to search and find scientific Web sites and highly technical medical information. The company was then able to sell subscriptions to this service, earning them $800,000 in the first six months.

"I'd also like to touch on how well our product can scale up to meet your future needs."

Next you'll give a description of the project, matching your core competencies to the requirements.

"We've come to see from our talks with your people that the primary requirement of the Derwent Categorization Project is the ability to categorize millions of patents automatically to enable your company to register and resell that information on a timely and profitable basis.

"Additionally, the application needs to scale across multiple computer platforms at your three facilities, needs to maintain a 97-percent uptime rate with in-house support only because the volume of work requires it, and needs to adapt easily to future requirements because the nature of your market is constantly changing. You'll see during this presentation that our software has proven accuracy and efficiency ratings in similar markets and has a fully customizable interface to link to your legacy system."

The remaining part of the presentation should focus on the solution and your product's role in it. You want to offer a good level of detail that shows how well you've listened and how much you've learned from discussions with the executive, the project manager, and the technical or service people. Use the client's terminology wherever possible, and reiterate your understanding of the requirements; this puts the client's people in an agreeable frame of mind.

"Our software scans an entire document and identifies key words and phrases about the subject matter. The results are compared against a master list of customer-supplied categories and tagged accordingly. The software also tracks unique concepts across documents, and once it reaches a sufficient number of hits, the software can even create a new category automatically."

The ultimate goal is to stimulate a lot of conversation on the client's side; the question-and-answer period of the presentation can go on for hours. As the emcee of the meeting, it's up to you to make sure someone is handed responsibility for every question that comes up that can't be dealt with immediately. For example, if one of your tech guys asks for a specific piece of information and the tech person who handles that area for the client says he'll have to check with his staff, you should pipe up with "OK, when you have that information, would you please call Joe about it?" If Joe doesn't hear back in 24 hours, he should start calling the client.

As the client's representatives are sitting there absorbing information about your product or service, they're already thinking of other ways to use it; this often means the actual project itself takes on a different form as you go through this meeting: "We already have someone to handle phase A, and it looks like you can't do phase B, which we thought you could handle. So, we want you to concentrate on phase C." While you're still at the table, get it all nailed down.

After you've shared ideas and come to solid conclusions, it's time to end the presentation and close for the preparation of the statement of work—the contract that lays out the details and cost of your solution. I usually wrap up by assuming the sale; even if the executive you originally met with can't be at the meeting, the project manager most likely has the authority and the budget to make the decision.

"Based on what we've discussed today, you've seen that our product delivers increased accuracy in analyzing and categorizing patent content. With a full implementation of our proposed solution, the return on investment is approximately six months. The next step for us is to build a statement of work together, finalize the roles both parties are going to play, and schedule a date to start the project."

When you've received their verbal approval, it's time to make your exit and immediately gather your team to debrief the call, just as you did with the Codebreaker after the first sales call. As the sales rep, you're going to offer your take on how well the members handled their portions of the presentation, then open up the floor for comment about both the current project and future presentations.

Now it's back to the office to put together the final proposal.

Chapter Checklist

To run an effective and successful second sales call, you have to:

☐ Aim for a date within two weeks after the first sales call.

☐ Invite the C-level exec you first met with, but if his schedule is proving difficult, forge ahead without him—don't lose momentum.

☐ Encourage as much information sharing as possible among your team members and the client's team members so that you can hone your presentation.

☐ Assign specific roles to each member of the team attending the call, and stage a rehearsal to iron out the kinks.

☐ Consider breaking your solution into phases to increase selling opportunities.

☐ Use your power as the emcee to maximize informative discussion between your team and the client's while keeping track of questions that need follow-up.

☐ Assume the sale and close for a contract/statement of work at the end of the call.

☐ Debrief your team immediately after the call to tie up loose ends and note areas for future improvement.

Preparing the Proposal/Statement of Work

A s I wrote in the last chapter, ideal second sales calls are wide-ranging conversations in which both client and vendor ask questions and kick around ideas. Even if you do manage to get down to specifics, it's hard to cover much in an hour or two. The result—in addition to securing the deal, of course—is usually the need for a conference call to hash out the contents of the proposal or statement of work.

For sellers of tangible goods, putting together a proposal isn't usually a very involved process; a list of units, prices, and deadlines will cover just about any deal. But consulting, with its huge scope, is a different story. Every project has at least some unique elements, and a detailed explanation of your proposed solution—a statement of work—is required.

Echoing the client's terminology wherever possible to establish a connection, a statement of work should relate your understanding of how the problem was presented, offer your analysis on the project the client has initiated to fix the problem, and detail your suggestions for making the project work. It goes on to list each side's responsibilities and deadlines, with a clear accounting of consulting fees, software and personnel costs, and expenses. Finally, it highlights a benchmark that signals a definitive end to the vendor's involvement in the project; otherwise you might find your-self in an expensive go-around with a client who wants "just one more series of quality assurance tests."

The more experienced your company is in a particular niche, the more likely it is that your team will have enough information to start work right after the call. If one of your goals is to market repeatable business solutions, it's a real time-saver to start with a generic statement of work that, after some minimal customization, you can send to the client for refining.

Parts of a Proposal/Statement of Work

Title Page

As silly as it sounds, make sure that you use the customer's name for the project as the title for your proposal. You wouldn't believe how many arguments I've gotten into over the years about this sim-ple and, from my experience, inarguable sales axiom: Wherever possible, use the customer's words, not your own. (For an illustra-tion of a typical title page, as well as sample text for each of the fol-lowing sections taken from an actual proposal, please see the Appendix at the back of the book.)

Client Overview

This section is an important paragraph or two relating a few basic facts about the client: the type of company (e.g., pharmaceutical, consumer product manufacturing, call center), an estimation of annual sales rev-enue, an approximate number of employees throughout the country or world (e.g., 14,000 employees in 12 countries), and key products or competencies. You might also list its biggest competitors and key focus. This information should be readily available from the client's Web site or PR department. You're not including this information for the client's benefit, naturally, but for your own executives and alliance partners who might not have a clear picture of the potential client.

Vendor Overview

This section, also a paragraph or two, lays out basic information on your company and product. It's not the place to put a broad-based commercial about what a great company you work for, with brochures and sales language. I've worked for companies that insisted on putting that kind of fluff at the beginning of proposals, and I've learned over the years that customers will just leaf past it as quickly as possible to get to your solution to the problem at hand.

Statement of Business Requirements

This is a detailed outline, anywhere from a paragraph to three-quarters of a page in length, of what the customer's require-ments are—precisely where help is needed. During a sales call, a good rep will actually ask the customer to state in his own words just what the project is. Even a pure hardware sale is still providing a solution; a copier doesn't just make black marks on paper, but helps a law firm process its court filing needs 20 per-cent faster.

If you managed to get the client's internal documentation on the project, as I suggested in Chapter 10, quote from it liberally in this section. Your client has thought through the requirements logi-cally and put them into words, probably after lots of debate—why put effort into a restatement that might end up backfiring on you?

Proposed Solution

Here's the heart of the statement of work. Though this portion is usually a page or less, it specifies the solution you are going to pro-vide. To begin, it should clearly mark out the start and the end of the project, both for billing purposes and for workflow management, in case you're just one part of a larger project.

The next step is explaining the scope of the project with a list that itemizes each stage of the solution and matches it to a time frame. Breaking the work down into logical phases and milestones like this allows you to craft what I call a "quick win" in the first phase—an opportunity to provide the client with an easily quantifiable return on investment in a short amount of time for a fraction of the total project cost. This, in turn, gives them greater confidence in your company's abilities and the entire future of the project.

Different vendors have different rules about how detailed this section should be—some are very reluctant to give out too much detail because they're afraid their clients are shopping around and saying: "Here you go; how much can you do this for? Can you beat $3 million?" If you have experience with the customer or have a good feel for the company's business practices, you can be pretty detailed here.

After the scope of the work, you should delineate what will be required of the client and at what times (e.g., "Client must provide an office or cubicle area and supply network passwords for five engineers on March 15th."). You will then list what equipment you will bring with you (e.g., "Vendor will supply network-ready laptops and extra storage media for backups.").

Costs

What the client sees is a short, straightforward list of costs by general category—hardware, software licenses, consulting services. Of course, you know that a lot of preparation has gone into coming up with these prices.

At this stage of the game, the sales rep has very little influence on pricing decisions—it's all in the hands of the finance guys now. But like a good math teacher, you want to see the calculations of what goes into the final price. Your team's project manager will be analyzing myriad details and making a time and cost accounting for each one: administrative overhead, the different consultants to be involved and over what period of time, how many weeks or months each phase of the project will take. As we discussed in Chapter 9, you as the sales rep will then contribute by costing out the tangible parts of the project such as hardware and software based on the team's guidelines and the manufacturers' price lists.

Once you have your internal breakdown from your team, you should always build in an extra 10 or 15 days of the combined price for all the labor before presenting the proposal to the client. This is the smartest way to handle "scope creep"—delays or complexities the customer didn't foresee in his analysis of the project. If you've already accounted for these inevitabilities, you can make almost any crisis look like a win-win situation by saying, "Sure, we can fix that without raising your price." The client will appreciate not having to go back to legal or to purchasing to get an extra $15,000 of work done. This practice also covers you in case some of the work wasn't estimated perfectly.

It's rare that you'll show the specific breakdown to the client—most just want the solution built and are therefore concerned only with your total time—but once in a while you will have one request; it in such a situation, it's good to have a copy prepared that already incorporates the differential in the line items (in other words, you don't want a line at the bottom saying "scope creep fudge factor"!).

Signature Page

Check with your company's legal department or counsel to determine how best to structure this page.

Addenda

This is the catch-all area for items that are important but don't have a direct bearing on the solution presented in the main portion of the proposal. The *terms and conditions*, for which you should again check with your legal department, list the client's general obligations, such as providing a safe working environment and adequate parking for your personnel. If you're selling a technological product or solution, the next addendum should reprint the *software licenses* for all the applications you're using as part of your solution, whether custom-made or off the shelf. Third, and most important from a sales and revenue standpoint, are *maintenance contracts.*

Maintenance contracts can be quite profitable but are often left out of proposals by both tangible goods salespeople and consultants alike. Big companies spend millions of dollars on maintenance contracts, which are generally priced at 15 to 20 percent of the original purchase price—on a million-dollar project, that's $150,000 to $200,000—per year, because if anything breaks, they want somebody to come out to fix it or replace it without delay. They can't afford to have downtime in a system that might be linked with five other critical systems throughout the company. And who better to maintain something than the company that put it together? Along these lines, maintenance contracts can be presented as differentiators: Tell the client you'll provide 24-hour-a-day access to a key engineer who will be onsite within three hours if there's a problem, and assure them that upgraded versions of software modules will be installed for free without forcing a system shutdown during business hours.

Every piece of equipment you sell and every solution you build should be bundled with a maintenance contract; if it's accepted by the client—and most are—such an arrangement guarantees you annual revenue. A maintenance contract renewed annually for the life of a product or system can end up exceeding the original fee. (Of course, you then need to task someone internally with tracking those contracts and sending out renewal notices 90 days before contract expiration; a small company I once worked with almost lost a million dollars in revenue because no one was keeping an eye on the maintenance contracts for its biggest customer.)

At the very end of the proposal, you can put brochures, white papers, and other sales materials that frequently aren't even read.

Client Review

The statement of work is never finalized until the customer has blessed it, and getting that approval is a back-and-forth process. When you have a rough draft ready for the client's team to review, send it with a cover letter stating that you believe the attached document represents everyone's best understanding of the project's premise and solution, but that you want their input at a conference call that you'd like to schedule for the morning three days from now. This gives them notice that they have to disseminate the document internally and discuss it. Often you'll get back e-mails pleading for more time; these are, of course, busy people, and unless the project is an emergency or other top priority, you're going to have to allow them the courtesy of dictating the timing of the conference call.

In the meantime, the project manager and her team will read it, discuss it among themselves, send e-mails to quiz your staff on certain aspects. Sometimes it's obvious that your teams have already established a great cooperative relationship and there are few points of difference, so you can allow the client to make the final changes in the document without a conference call. But because a conference call is fairly typical, that's how we'll begin the next chapter.

Chapter Checklist

To prepare a winning proposal, you have to:

☐ Echo your client's terminology whenever possible.

☐ Keep the introductory material short—it's the solution that everyone is interested in.

☐ Break your solution down into realistic phases and milestones.

☐ Build an extra 10 to 15 days of labor costs into your price to mitigate the effects of scope creep.

☐ Include a maintenance contract provision.

The Decision-Makers' Conference Call and the Close

We've reached the last steps of an intense process that has brought you from initial market research to a million-dollar contract in one to three months. It's often said that the last 10 percent of any undertaking is the hardest to complete, but if you've been working hard and truly listening to your customers all along, you'll find that the culminating week of a big deal generally moves swiftly and smoothly.

Based on the feedback your team received from the client's core team on the rough draft of the proposal or statement of work, they can now complete their final draft. Before delivering this to the client, it makes sense to send it around to three or four people internally who haven't been directly involved, such as the managers of your tactical team members and a high-level executive, and ask them to review it overnight; you'll always get a better document if other eyes see it to catch a typo here or some bad math over there. Then, when it's *final* final, e-mail it to everyone on the client's side who's been involved, from the CEO down—no matter how trustworthy the client's project manager is, don't trust him to disseminate the proposal.

In fact, one of the main reasons to schedule a decision-maker's conference call is that, even though you've made sure the document has wide dissemination, it might have proven impossible for the client's entire decision-making team to discuss it. The call is the spur to do this; I've often heard that after I've scheduled a call for 10:00 a.m., the project manager immediately schedules a meeting one hour earlier to make sure her side has done their homework. In fact, you might want to set up a time and date for this call right *before* sending out the proposal—it helps to move things along if the client's team knows they need to review the material quickly. As I noted at the end of the last chapter, however, sometimes you might have to bow to the client's time constraints and reschedule. But always press for the earliest date you can.

Whether it's a Web-based conference or just a multiparty phone conference, the setup is simple. You're not there to impress the client all over again—except with your efficiency. Have only absolutely necessary team members on the line with you; the project director or another mid-level manager will be running the client's side of the call. Your technical or service representatives are going to run your part of the show, but you can help direct the conversation with instant messaging: "Make sure you mention X." "Don't talk about Y." (Just don't forget to turn down the notification chime!)

Kick off the call by highlighting your focus: to determine whether the essence of the project is properly represented in the document. Start with a brief mention of the client and vendor overviews and then put the ball in their court by asking if there are any changes necessary.

"The object of today's conference call is to review the statement of work for the Verizon E-Billing Project and see what suggestions you have about it. Before we talk about the specifics, do you have any questions about the overview paragraphs?"

Move on to summarizing the business requirements of the project, and ask after each one if all agree that it represents what's needed.

"This project needs to enable Verizon's 9 million customers to retrieve and pay their monthly bills online by integrating a state-of-the-art Web interface with a back-end UNIX system. Are there any new requirements we should be made aware of at this time?"

Then turn it over to your technical or service team to do the same with each action item in the statement of work or proposal.

"I'm going to give the floor to Scott, who will walk us through phase one of the project."

You can get a feel for what level of detail the customer's team wants to engage in at this point and adjust if necessary. Generally, there shouldn't be too much conversation about the actual project; you're touching lightly on points and affirming understanding. It's possible—and quite likely if you've made a real effort to address their concerns over the past few days—that the call might come down to the clarification of just one or two items.

If the customer throws up a flag, let him frame the question in his own words. As soon as he says "Now, about item 12," your staff is going to want to jump right in with their own explanations, but hold them back until the exact issue is identified and make sure they speak only to the point raised. Don't be surprised if the questions revolve around something as small as one word—you hope the information sharing you've done before this conference call takes care of such things, but it's possible the two people who care most deeply about the issue haven't had a chance to bump into each other in the hall yet.

The only exception to the "speak only when spoken to" tactic above is when there are opportunities to plant a seed for future projects. As you're going over the items one by one, it's easy for one of your team members—briefed on this ahead of time, of course—to bring a project growth opportunity into the conversation:

"Speaking of item 9, I just wanted to mention that the security module could easily be modified down the road to interface with offsite systems."

Again, this is not the time for the hard sell, and it's not something you want to append to each and every item on the statement of work; you're simply presenting information that you can follow up on once the project is under way.

Even if there is some heavy discussion, the call shouldn't last more than an hour. Occasionally there will be someone who is obviously reading the document for the first time and keeps asking you to go back to items that everyone else agrees have already been settled. My advice in such a situation is to answer the questions as briefly as possible and keep pressing forward; usually, after two or three interruptions, his own people will make their displeasure known and he'll quiet down.

Potential Problems

Unless there's been a major breakdown of communication between the teams or within the client's team, it's rare for this final call to go really wrong, but that doesn't mean there aren't some curveballs. What I've learned about many types of projects is that they're evolutionary, constantly changing through no fault of the customer. In just the few days between delivering a draft of a statement of work and the final conference call, new information can crop up that alters some aspect of the scope of the work. You might be treated to some unexpected news, such as "One thing we forgot to mention before is that our plant closes down the last two weeks of August each year, and we'll need more perimeter security during that time." You get used to surprises—and it's why you should always anticipate "scope creep" in your pricing.

Another common problem is a sudden budget cut that drastically affects the scope. And it's not as if your customer's team is holding information back just to spring it on you at the last minute— they might have found out themselves just the hour before the meeting. This, again, is why it's so important to conceive projects in phases—if the money available dries up without warning, you can still complete key areas and leave the client satisfied. A solid win, even in a single phase, can often make the difference between receiving funding for additional work and being left out in the cold.

Remember to understand that your clients are frustrated, overworked, brilliant, maxed out—they've got 55 balls in the air and they have to keep them going smoothly. A bit of empathy in these situations, and calm in the face of chaos, goes a long way to cementing working partnerships.

Sometimes customers will also use this opportunity to ask for a few more things at the same price, using the looming close as a negotiating lever. This is yet another reason to build in a cushion during the writing of the statement of work; you can now throw in an extra service or two and make yourself look flexible without seriously affecting your bottom line.

Wrapping Up the Call

When the client requests a change, your team should be able to say immediately whether it will affect the project in a significant way. If it's minor, make the change there at the table. If it will have larger ramifications, open it up to discussion; if all agree it's necessary, you will have to send a revised statement of work that might have a recalculated price. Unless the entire thrust of the project has been redirected, you shouldn't have to schedule a new conference call—the revisions can just be run past the responsible party on the client's side.

Assuming there are no big changes to deal with, once you've completed the group review of the statement of work, the deal is essentially done. Ask the project manager or director to sign the signature page of the statement of work and fax it over to you.

Undoubtedly he'll reply that his signature is worthless until he has a purchase order approved. You'll respond that you know a purchase order will have to be issued before anything can proceed, but a signature will enable you to reserve the resources and personnel necessary on your side to undertake the work. The signature is really a symbol of mutual trust.

If there are some changes necessary, end the call with a promise to get the project director the final revised document as soon as possible. As a sales rep you should never publicly tie your people down with a specific time. When you hang up the phone and talk to your team, it might turn out that something the customer asked for that seemed minor to you will actually have a ripple effect throughout your solution. Use a quick postcall debriefing to examine any remaining issues and assign responsibility for resolving them.

By the time the hour is getting short, this kind of call usually gets pretty informal. There's often a lot of fun talk about getting started and where the project might lead. After all the hard thinking and discussion, there's an excitement in the air. But it's not time to celebrate quite yet.

The Close

The modern-day deal closing isn't like the old movies in which grinning business tycoons in high-backed chairs brandish fancy pens while their underlings applaud behind them—there's too much work to be done to waste that much time. Really, the close today is just an anticlimactic waiting period. You have the project manager's signature on the statement of work, and now you're waiting for the document to clear your respective legal departments so that it can move to purchasing.

Legal's not usually much of a hurdle, but it can take awhile; the lawyers have to justify their existence somehow, right? If you have a pretty good feeling early in the selling process that the project or contract will likely go forward, you can try to preclear with the client's legal department whatever terms and conditions are necessary for the product you're supplying or the solution you're building, and then run their changes by your own counsel. (In fact, the worst trouble I ever had was with someone in my own legal department. The lawyer wouldn't budge on some intellectual property issues—which we had no right claiming in the first place—and we lost the deal. You'd better believe my boss made sure that didn't happen the next time a similar deal came up.) If you manage to get this out of the way, the review of the final document should take a lot less time. Otherwise, you just have to be patient and politely ask for updates.

It's a similar situation in regard to the purchase order, which is the real marker of the successful close. Unless a project is extremely urgent, purchase orders usually take two or three weeks after legal approval to come through, and there's not a lot you can do to hurry it along except stay in touch with the project manager or director and offer to intervene if there are any snags. Until the purchase order is cut, some clients might try some of the hardball tactics I've mentioned previously: coming back and asking for another 10 percent off, trying to get a new piece of the project included in the quoted price, even deciding to take your statement of work and use it as the blueprint for an internal team to build the solution.

You can't really do anything about that kind of negotiating, but if you're getting squeezed on price and you're protected by the fudge factor I recommended, you can turn it to your advantage by pressing for something in return and preclosing—"OK, if I'm able to get that discount for you, can I get the purchase order next Monday?" Ask for something to prove the discount is valuable. Of course, you have to have a sense of whether the customer is someone you can deal with, who will feel a sense of obligation when you manage to shave $20,000 off the price at the last minute.

Sometimes they might just ask to start the project sooner— customers often go slowly until they make a final decision, and then want vendors to start work the next day. You know it usually isn't possible to grant this request completely because the resources are committed elsewhere, but it's worth checking in with your staff to see if anyone can be shifted over right away to at least begin the new project.

But once that purchase order finally shoots its way out of the client's accounting system, you've really done it—you've made a million-dollar deal in two sales calls. Your customers are happy, your bosses are happy, your Codebreaker is happy, you've got an impressive commission check coming your way, and you now have a vast new arsenal of techniques to use. Our last chapter will look at the best ways to leverage your new success in the pursuit of even greater business goals.

Chapter Checklist

To pave the way for a smooth close, you have to:

☐ Send the final draft of your proposal or statement of work around internally for a last once-over.

☐ Take on the responsibility of disseminating the final document to everyone who needs to see it on the client's side.

☐ Schedule the final conference call as soon as you can after sending out the document, but be flexible if the client really needs more time.

☐ Be patient if unexpected scope questions or budgetary problems suddenly crop up.

☐ Get a signature on the document at the end of the conference call.

☐ Try to have precleared as much as possible with your own and your client's legal departments.

☐ Be ready for a last-minute negotiating attempt by the client as you both wait for the purchase order to be processed.

Repeat Business: Picking the Low-Hanging Fruit

You've closed your first million-dollar deal with a new client. Because you've done your homework at every step and managed the details so well, the process went beautifully, and your team is eager to set up shop and do a great job. Clearly, a client who needed a solution of such magnitude is an excellent prospect for more business; sometimes you'll already have identified additional projects during one of your sales calls or in conversation with a project manager. But most of the time, you'll have no clear map of where this client relationship will go. Knowing that it's 10 times harder to crack into a new account from scratch than to penetrate and radiate next door, or to another department in the same company, how soon can you go back to this particular well?

Many sales reps will immediately enter full attack mode to drum up other business, and that's very brazen. Because the customer hasn't even worked with you, she might flat out refuse, which will cast a pall on your budding relationship. Even if she does agree to help you, her discomfort will likely show in a lukewarm or hesitant recommendation.

It's much better to have completed a healthy portion of the project before leveraging a new contact, perhaps halfway or three-quarters through a project on which your team is doing a superb job. More aggressive reps will argue this point, but in my experience, a client has to feel very familiar and friendly before he's open to hearing "Would you introduce me to somebody else in your company that I could work with?" Figuring out the best time to pop that question is really an art. You're waiting for a wave of good feeling, when two or three things have happened that make him realize you're doing great things for him and for his company—and that his own value will rise if he trumpets those successes.

But it's not as if you'll always have to wait months for the right opportunity to ask someone to walk you down the hall. A project of almost any length will give you lots of chances to meet other people while touching base with your main contact. In fact, you can start to build a client base just by attending some of the technical meetings prompted by your project. No matter what your product or service, it's almost a certainty that it will affect multiple departments and processes within the client's organization. Everybody with a stake in the project will have to come together at least a few times a month to analyze the ramifications and progress of the undertaking. Your team members, who are essentially employees of the client's company for a certain time, will be right there with them. They are your ticket in—use them!

When a job starts, you have to decide whether to accompany your staff on the first day. Even though you're not going to build anything, you want to show that you're involved in this solution—after all, you're the one who found the project and closed the deal. There's a fine balance to be struck between pursuing other sales and putting your best foot forward in a brand-new account; if you think there's a good likelihood of expanding the account, go for an hour or two to kick things off and get some first impressions of the personnel from other departments you want to work with in the future.

After that first day, you're going to rely on the staff on site to keep you informed, not only about the milestones in the statement of work and when they're being reached, but also when the big meetings are taking place. Tell them you want a heads-up even if they think you're booked solid; I used to happily reschedule something internally to have a chance to get to know more of the client's project managers and their current needs.

Be aware that sometimes it takes a little finesse to get into these larger meetings. A sales rep isn't always a welcome face, especially when there are heated issues expected on the table. My advice is never to ask permission—just go; you've already established that you're part of the team. Have one of your guys, not the client, meet you in the lobby and take you down to the conference room. Your cover will be blown when you see the project manager, of course, but your relationship should be at the point where he'll know that on this day you're there to learn, not to sell. (That comes the next day when you ring up all the managers you met!)

Other Methods of Making Connections

Personal recommendations are undoubtedly the best way to radiate within an account, but if you're in a holding pattern waiting for the right moment, there are a few other approaches to try.

The first thing is to go back and review the notes from your original sales call with your C-level contact. See whether there are other projects you can follow up on, or names that you might have put aside in pursuit of the most promising project. If you find that you have a project description with no name attached, the project manager you're currently working with or her boss the director can probably fill you in. You could also use this situation as an opportunity to reconnect with the CIO by sending him a copy of the statement of work and an update on your team's progress. Once he has a chance to evaluate your competence, he will be more likely to give you the names that match up to the projects you touched on in the original sales call, and even pass along your name once again.

Another possibility: Ask one of your team members working on site to obtain a client personnel directory—as he'll have an easier time getting it than you would as a sales rep. Once you have it, you can make some quick, low-key calls to others within the company: "I'm working for John Doe down the hallway. We're doing a knowledge management project I wanted to make you aware of. Is there any interest in that kind of capability for the projects that you might have?" People like to be filled in on what's transpiring around them, and by keeping your tone open and informational, you'll find a receptive audience.

Finally, one of the subtle things I like to encourage when doing work at a new client is having our staff wear shirts with the company logo. The branding identifies them in meetings and catches the eye of people in the hallways, leading to the two questions salespeople most like to hear: "Who are those guys?" and "What are they doing?"

Preparing Metrics and Other Marketing Materials

As you work to develop new business from this huge deal, other departments in your company will want to highlight your achievements for their own purposes. Larger companies employ a staff of marketing professionals to collect and disseminate this information, but you should not rely on them for your own needs.

Now, don't get me wrong—it's great to have an active marketing department that announces your latest successes to the trade press and assembles case studies for potential clients to review. But the more complex or innovative the solution your team has developed, the less the marketers truly understand it. Because you're already looking for proof sources, such as cost and manpower savings and revenue enhancements, that you can incorporate into your talk tracks and your 30-second commercial, it's more efficient and beneficial to do it yourself.

Once my staff has entered the testing/quality assurance phase on a project, I start asking the client's project manager or director whether any quantitative results are available. Usually they aren't ready yet—it's typical for projects to undergo an internal review before any conclusions are drawn—but the manager will have a pretty good idea of when they will be. I'll try to book an appointment right then so that he knows upfront that I really want those metrics.

Other times I'll encounter clients who don't want to share the information, but not because it's a trade secret—all too often, they simply haven't bothered to go back and figure out how quantitatively successful the project was. People at the top of the company whose job it is to think strategically should *want* closure to a project, to hear from their staff how the execution went and what the results were. I wish I understood the mindset behind the reluctance to delve into this because everybody loves to hear these numbers beforehand in the sales call.

Of course, not all projects are that simple: They take years to implement fully, or affect so many areas in a company that it's nearly impossible to get a handle on hard numbers. But in most cases, to get usable information you'll need to ask leading questions, as though you were in court: "Would you say this project saved you 20 percent on your development costs? Well, would you say 10 percent?" or "Did you save 300 man-hours of work a month? How about 200?" You don't need to pin them down to a specific number for each metric; a reasonably close range is fair enough for your future sales pitches.

Don't make the mistake of missing the things that can't be measured but are just as valuable—something that makes a company a voice rather than an echo in the marketplace. In the late 1990s, a company I worked for was an integral part of getting the Volkswagen Beetle sold online. Web-based car shopping is almost routine now, but back then no one had ever done it before. Enabling a client to initiate a business revolution might not translate directly into dollars and cents, but the impression created by such an achievement can open a lot of doors for client and vendor alike.

Once you've made sense of the metrics and any intangibles, you can pass them along to the marketing department to be combined with descriptions of the project's requirements and outcomes for a case study. These short solution narratives are not universally read, but a certain kind of analytical customer loves them, especially if your company has a reputation for including solid information. For this reason, it's important to include clauses in the terms and conditions section of your proposals or statements of work that allow you to use your clients' names in marketing materials and request an on-the-record testimonial. (Be aware that a client's legal department will occasionally ask that such conditions be taken out or insist on reserving approval by their own marketing or communications department before anything is released.) Ultimately, when the case study is complete and in your hands, it gives you another opening to call up the C-level executive: "I wanted to thank you again for going with us for the XYZ project, and I'd like to send this to you to show you what the results were."

Remember, though, that all the numbers in the world aren't always as effective as a satisfied customer who agrees to become a "friendly" you call on when a potential new client needs some first-hand information about you and your product or service before committing to a sales call. After a project has gone well, sound out the project manager or director you're closest to and ask if she'd be willing to answer a few questions about the solution you provided: What other vendors did you look at for the project, and why did you pick us? How did our team work for you? How was our customer service? Then see if she'd mind being called on from time to time to talk about it with someone from a noncompetitive market. It's a rare client whose expectations you've exceeded who won't be willing to share a success story.

Go Forth and Be a Codebreaker

We've reached the end of what I hope will be a regular and profitable companion in your selling career. Once you've done a few deals with Codebreakers, the process becomes second nature. It will start to become difficult for you *not* to see multiple opportunities from almost every meeting and to share great information and leads with your fellow reps.

As you gain experience with million-dollar deals and make inroads at large clients, you too will be in the position to act as a Codebreaker—not only for colleagues in the office but for hungry salespeople with fresh ideas at other companies who see the value of the Codebreaker system. I urge you to spread the word—and the success—everywhere you can. Together, by infusing sales with the spirit of cooperation, we can identify, propose, and deliver faster and better business solutions to clients—and exceed our own goals with a speed we never thought possible. Happy selling!

Chapter Checklist

To make the most of your million-dollar deal, you have to:

☐ Finish a respectable portion of the project before asking your customer for new business.

☐ Reach out to other client departments by accompanying your team members to project strategy meetings.

☐ Review your notes from the original sales call to see if there are other potential projects you can now follow up on.

☐ Take the time to go back and compile metrics as the project winds up—these become your case studies and ROI talking points with future clients.

☐ Use your new skills to become a Codebreaker yourself and spread the wealth!

Sample Proposal

Proposal for ABC Company, Inc.

CLIENT OVERVIEW

About ABC Company

ABC Company has been in the business of publishing direc-
tories since 1932 in book form or on CD-ROM. The CD-ROM
also contains up-to-date real estate information that is used
primarily by key industries like insurance, government, home
services, mortgage, and real estate. The current customer
base for the CD-ROM product is more than 4500.

ABC Company key objectives are to find a simplistic way
to make the real estate application available through another
medium, namely the Internet. The solution should be designed
in a manner that it retains the functionality and screens and
maximum code reuse from the existing application. The solution should also cater to back-end administration functionality,
software installation on the client side, etc.

VENDOR OVERVIEW

About XYZ Company

XYZ Company is a technology-focused company providing e-engineering solutions to its customers, utilizing its strong expertise in the areas of Internet middleware, database, data warehouse, and XML technologies.

Since the company started its operations in 1996, it has focused exclusively in the database and data warehouse and middleware technologies, working with clients such as Microsoft, Ardent Software (now Informix), and IBM Almaden Research Center. With the growth of the Internet, XYZ Company positioned itself as a leading provider of software infrastructure and business integration solutions for the emerging Internet economy space with a sharp market focus on the Enterprises and B2B market segments. XYZ Company is currently 425 people strong, having offices throughout the United States.

STATEMENT OF BUSINESS REQUIREMENTS

Requirements Overview

This section contains an overview of the total project requirements as understood at the time of this proposal preparation and is for discussion purposes. It is based on the "Request for Proposal–ZKD Internet Product" document dated August 31, 2001 provided by ABC Company.

A Statement of Work document will be subsequently prepared at the end of the requirements analysis phase and describes the specifics of the work, agreed to activities, the schedules, the deliverables, and budgets.

Project Goals

The main objective of ABC Company is to make their existing real estate information available over the Internet. At the same time, they want to retain the existing look and feel of the screens because of the large percentage of their customer base using the existing CD-ROM product. They also want to protect the large investments made in developing and supporting the existing CD-ROM product.

High-level Functional Requirements

1. Convert the existing CD-ROM application into an Internet-based application. Currently the CD-ROM application uses a database stored on the local hard drive as the data repository. This needs to be modified to have the data residing on a central server and let the application run

searches on the server using the Internet as a medium to transfer data between the local machine and the centralized database server.

2. Search functionality and saving of search criteria for future use.

3. Conversion utility to load the configuration of the existing customers to the server side.

4. View of the search results as customized by the user.

5. Support for exporting of records.

6. Transfer of program data, which includes basic county, transfer, and mortgage data.

7. Automatic software updates using the Internet.

8. DNC/DNM/restricted lists.

9. Save Farm Areas, Remarks, Export of Records.

10. Back-end administration functionality covering the password management, turning on/off of services and four-tiered access management.

11. Back-end reporting on system utilization.

Technical Requirements

1. **Performance**: The Internet product should mimic the performance of the CD-ROM applications. It is XYZ Company's endeavor to deliver an application that will perform, well but the performance cannot be guaranteed because of network dependencies.

2. **Security**: As sensitive data is being exchanged, the solution should provide strict authentication/access control. All sensitive information would be protected during the transfer from

browser/application to server and vice-versa using HTTPS. Access to various features of the application should be controlled depending on the permissions given to the users.

3. **Standards-based architecture**: All the technologies used in the solution should be standards based so that it will be easy for the clients and third-party solutions providers to hook up to the solution using standard components.

4. **Scalability**: The solution should be designed to handle a number of concurrent users. Also, it should be possible to dynamically increase the configuration so that increased load can be handled.

5. **Reusability**: Wherever possible, the solution should reuse the existing components that are available with the CD-ROM application.

6. **Server Administration module should be fully Web enabled**: The administrative users of the solution should be able to interact with the application using Internet Explorer 5.0 or higher, both from within and outside the firewall.

Acceptance Criteria

The core set of acceptance criteria should be defined by ABC Company at the end of the detailed requirements phase. This should be mutually agreed upon between ABC Company and XYZ Company. It should cover functional requirements that form the core application as well as nonfunctional requirements like UI look and feel, scalability, and performance.

PROPOSED SOLUTION

Our Proposed Solution

Application Flow

A very high-level application flow is described below.

- The client application is either downloaded from the Web site or shipped via a CD-ROM and installed on the desktop.

- The application is invoked from the desktop and the user is authenticated with a username/password on the server by initiating the SOAP request from the client application.

- Once the user is authenticated successfully, the list of all counties subscribed and licensed by the user will be sent as a response to the client application.

- The client application can choose a county and start working on the search criteria.

- The index data for all the search criteria is already stored on the local hard disk. This information is stored onto the local hard disk either as a transfer from the Web site or using the CD-ROM that has been shipped to the customer.

- Once the user has finalized the search criteria and pressed the process button, the list of all parcel numbers satisfying the search criteria will be determined on the client side, and that list will be sent as a SOAP request to the server side.

- The services running on the server side will fetch the detailed parcel data for all parcel numbers from the Real estate SQL Server database and send the response back to the client application.

- The client application will then display the search result details in the customized format. The user can also export the data to the local hard disk in the different file formats that are available. The map-related information is also stored on the client side.

- The user is allowed to save the farm areas, remarks, search criteria, etc., onto the server.

Given below is a more detailed explanation of the various components of the solution.

Internet Application

This is the modified version of the current CD-ROM application that is available and would be used to access the data from the server. The application runs on the client side (desktop) accessing the real estate data residing on the server side. This application will retain the look and feel of the screens that are available with the current CD-ROM application. The Internet application will be a modified version of the existing VB application that uses Simple Object Access Protocol (SOAP) protocol to communicate with the server. It also uses HTTPS for securing the transmission of data over the Internet. On the server side, the services are deployed as COM components under MTS. Each of the services would perform the basic operations such as Insert, Update, Delete, and View operations, in addition to some business logic on the resources it is acting on.

Server Administration Application

This is the application component that is used by the marketing and server administration personnel of ABC

Company to configure and modify the parameters of the solution. This can be accessed both from within and outside the firewall. The server administration module is also used to define the various roles to the members of the ABC Company marketing and technical teams and thus the access permissions to the various reports that are available. The application would be developed using the ASP technology, written as COM objects enclosed in a Microsoft Transaction Server container.

Data Repositories

There are two data repositories. The first would be the Real Estate Data, which is the data that is being merchandised by ABC Company. The second repository has the data about the customers and the transactions they perform. The customer information would be accessible only by the ABC Company administrative and technical personnel with the appropriate access rights. This information would be used by the Reports Engine to generate the activity and utilization reports. All the data, both Real Estate and the Customer Information, would reside in a Microsoft SQL Server 7.0 database as mandated in the RFP document.

Reports Engine

The Reports Engine is a module that consists of the business logic to generate the reports as defined in the requirements document. This reports engine would be designed in such a way that new reports could be added to the suite of reports that are available.

Auxiliary Modules

This set of modules is designated for the purpose of the administration and updating of the client side application code and client data as specified in the RFP document. The module to convert CD-ROM data into the server side data and the module to move the current customer search information into the server are the other auxiliary modules that would be developed as part of the project.

COSTS

Commercial Proposal

Total Estimated Project Cost

The total project cost, based on discussions to date, is estimated to be $1,830,450. Please refer to Appendix 3 for the detailed breakdown of cost per phase of the project. Also refer to the attached rate sheet for the hourly rates of the various profiles of the resources.

PROFILE OF THE RESOURCE/WORK	RATES
Onsite Requirements Analysis by XYZ Company Development Manager/ Architect (ABC Company site)	$255/hr + per diem charges+ travel expenses
Onsite Development, Testing, Training and Deployment Work by XYZ Company Developers (ABC Company site)	$255/hr + per diem charges + travel expenses
Project Management/Design/Architecture by XYZ Company Development Manager/Architect	$180/hr
Development/Maintenance and Testing by XYZ Company Development and QA Engineers	$180/hr
Support, Documentation, Help Desk Support by XYZ Company Resources	$120/hr

- Travel Expenses are billed at $2000/visit for every visit to ABC Company site.

- Per Diem charges are billed at $150/day of stay at ABC Company site.

- Work is assumed to be at 40 hrs per week or 8 hrs per day.

Payment Terms

- 20-percent advance at the time of the signing of the contract.

- 20 percent at the end of the Requirements gathering phase and signing of the Statement of Work.

- 20 percent at the end of the Design phase of the project.

- 20 percent at the end of the Deployment Testing phase of the project.

- 10 percent at the end of Acceptance Testing phase of the project.

- 10 percent at the end of the User Training phase of the project.

Contract and Licensing Agreements

XYZ Company and ABC Company would sign a Master Service Agreement (MSA) and a Nondisclosure Agreement (NDA), attached in Appendix 4, which would determine and govern the business relationship between the two companies. All engagements, the current and the future, would then be under the purview of the MSA. At the end of the detailed requirements analysis phase, the Statement of Work (SOW), template attached as Appendix 4, would be signed off on. The Statement of Work would determine the scope of the work, the exact cost estimates, the project plan and the acceptance criteria for the solution.

[Signature page and addenda should follow with your specific legal language.]

INDEX

About the Authors

Patricia Gardner is a proven sales expert with an impressive record of breaking into Fortune 100 companies and making million-dollar deals in record time. Since her career began at Xerox in 1973, Patricia has distinguished herself in sales management, training, and consulting. She has used the *Million Dollar Sale* approach to close million-dollar deals at some of the largest corporations in America, including Honeywell, Sears, Verizon, Goodyear, TransAmerica, and Johnson & Johnson. Patricia is a popular author, consultant, and speaker. For more information, visit her Web site at www.maximumsales.com.

Timothy Haas writes about business, travel, and personal finance from southern New Jersey.